LETTS HOME DECORATOR

FLOORS
& TILES

LETTS HOME DECORATOR

FLOORS
& TILES

DAVID HOLLOWAY
AND
FRED MILSON

NEW
HOLLAND

This edition first published in 1996 by
New Holland (Publishers) Ltd
London • Cape Town • Sydney • Singapore

24 Nutford Place
London W1H 6DQ
UK

P.O. Box 1144
Cape Town 8000
South Africa

3/2 Aquatic Drive
Frenchs Forest, NSW 2086
Australia

ISBN 1 85238 380 1 (hbk)
ISBN 1 85368 736 7 (pbk)

Editorial Director: Joanna Lorenz
Project Editor: Judith Simon
Text Editor: Charles Moxham
Design: Millions Design
Cover design: Peter Crump
Photographer: John Freeman
Illustrator: King & King Associates

Designed and edited by
Anness Publishing Ltd
1 Boundary Row
London SE1 8HP

Printed and bound in Singapore by Tien Wah Press (Pte) Ltd

PUBLISHER'S NOTE
The authors and publisher have made every effort to ensure
that all instructions contained within this book are accurate
and safe, and cannot accept liability for any resulting injury,
damage or loss to persons or property however it may arise.
If in any doubt as to the correct procedure to follow for any
home improvements task, seek professional advice.

CONTENTS

INTRODUCTION

The floors in the home have a tough time. You want them to look good, but at the same time expect them to withstand furniture being dumped on them (and moved around) and to act as a general purpose surface on which to live, work, dance, play and generally move around.

This book looks at all aspects of floors: how they are constructed, how they can get damaged, how they are repaired and, above all, the many ways to make them look good using a wide variety of floor coverings, including woodstrip, carpet, vinyl, cork and stone and ceramic tiles.

But the book is not just about floors and floor coverings; the other half of the title is 'tiles', which you can use on walls as well as on floors. Ceramic tiles, cork tiles, mirror tiles and the rest can all be used both decoratively in living rooms and bedrooms and functionally in kitchens and bathrooms to provide a surface which is attractive, hardwearing and easy to keep clean.

Detailing the choice of floor coverings and tiles which are available and outlining some basic skills, this book will enable you to plan and coordinate your chosen materials with other design features in your home – to provide colour, texture, mood and style. You will also discover, in step-by-step detail, what is involved in carrying out the various jobs, from re-laying a timber floor to laying stair carpet and tiling around obstructions on walls.

The photographs and illustrations on the following pages will give you an idea of what can be achieved. If you follow the advice given, you will be able to turn your own redecorating dreams into an equally accomplished reality.

Modern vinyl floor tiles can give a whole range of realistic effects – here, the appearance of a woodblock floor in American oak.

BASIC TOOLS AND EQUIPMENT

On this page are shown some of the basic tools and equipment you will need when tackling flooring and tiling. Some of these you may already own; some would be worth purchasing for future reuse; some specialist tools can be hired when necessary.

These are not all the tools you will need: other tools and equipment for specific jobs are described in the relevant chapters and sections.

1 Electric drill You will need some kind of electric drill, mainly for making holes in walls and floors. This is a cordless drill, which also doubles as an electric screwdriver. The detachable battery pack is recharged in the **charging unit** (2) – it is worth having two battery packs, so one can be charging while the other one is in use.

3 Drill bits You will need a selection of twist drill bits, plus masonry drill bits for drilling into solid walls and floors to fit **screws** (4) and **wallplugs** (5).

6 Angle grinder For cutting and grinding masonry (and metal), it is mainly used in flooring and tiling for shaping tough tiles, such as quarry tiles (using a masonry grinding disc). It may also be used (with a masonry cutting disc) for cutting into solid concrete or a brick wall. It can be hired.

7 Disc sander This is a rubber backing plate which can be fitted to an angle grinder and which takes circular **sanding discs** (8). It is useful for sanding down wood or wall filler when removing a fair amount of material.

9 Eye protectors and **gloves** (10) These must always be worn when using tools such as an angle grinder.

11 Portable workbench An essential piece of equipment that provides a working surface (for cutting tiles, for example) in the room where you are working. It can be used both as a flat platform and as a large vice for holding materials.

12 Spirit level Used to determine true verticals and horizontals – especially when marking out batten (furring strip) positions in preparation for tiling. Can also be used as a metal straight-edge.

13 Coping saw Useful for cutting curves and slots in wood – especially when fitting floorboards around awkward objects such as pipes.

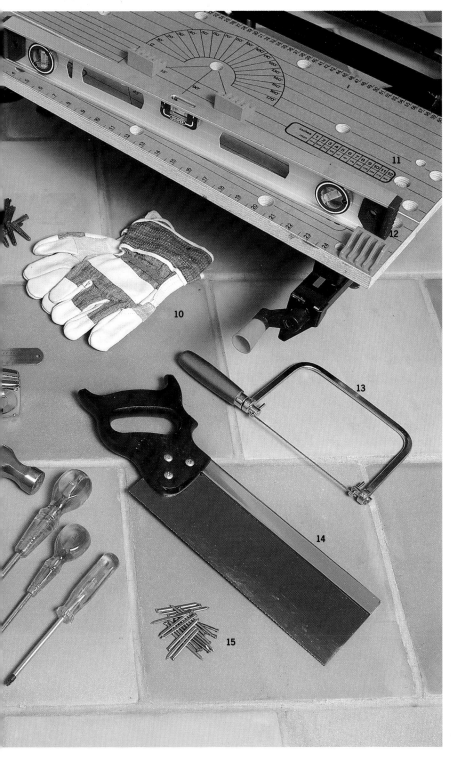

15 Masonry nails You will need some of these for holding guide battens in place when tiling walls. Wear eye protectors when hammering them in as they can fly out of the wall unexpectedly.

16 Screwdrivers A selection of screwdrivers is needed for flooring and tiling jobs, including at least one cross-head screwdriver to match modern screws.

17 Hammer This is essential for nailing down floorboards, putting in masonry nails and various other jobs. Choose a 'claw' hammer as shown here which can also be used for extracting nails.

18 Tape measure A steel retractable tape measure is essential. Choose one at least 3 m (10 ft) long – or, preferably, 5 m (16 ft) long. Do not attempt to measure accurately with a cloth tape measure.

19 Steel rule This doubles as a way of measuring small distances and as a straight-edge for cutting cork tiles with a trimming knife. For making longer cuts – in, say, lino or vinyl sheet – you will need a longer steel straight-edge, though you could use the edge of a long metal spirit level (**12**).

20 Try square A try square has its steel blade set exactly at right angles to its wooden handle and is used in two ways: one for checking that two surfaces are square to one another (the vertical and horizontal guide battens used for tiling walls, for example); the other for marking a cutting line with a **pencil** (**21**) square to a surface – such as on the end of a floorboard.

22 Trimming knife A really sharp trimming knife is the best way of cutting soft floor coverings and sheet material such as hardboard. Always use the retractable type of knife so that the blade can be slid away after use; the **smaller knife** shown (**23**) has 'snap-off' blades so that you can always have a truly sharp edge.

14 Tenon saw (backsaw) Not the fastest way of cutting wood, but one of the most accurate. It is essential for trimming timber floor coverings (such as mosaic) and for cutting small battens.

For cutting floorboards and flooring joists to length, a panel saw is a better tool.

PREPARATION

When the time comes to replace or change a floor covering, this is the perfect opportunity to check that your floors are structurally sound, looking for signs of localized damage, woodworm infestations and ensuring that the surface is level. Indeed, whatever floor covering you choose, whether it is soft carpeting or cushioned sheet flooring, or hard ceramic or stone tiles, you will not achieve the first-rate effect you seek without careful preparation. This chapter looks at floor structures in general, advises on identifying possible problems and outlines repair strategies for all types of floors including stairs.

Before laying any new floor covering – such as this classic woodstrip floor – the sub-floor requires meticulous preparation to ensure it is dry, level and flat.

ASSESSING THE SITUATION

Before deciding what needs to be done to your floors and the best way to treat them, it helps if you understand how floors are constructed – the different materials used and the ways they are put together.

Floors can be divided into two sorts: solid and suspended.

SOLID FLOORS

A solid floor is what it says: solid. It consists of a sand and cement *screed* laid over a solid concrete *slab*, which in turn sits on a *hardcore base*. Hardcore is the name given to a mixture of stones, clean broken brick and gravel which evens out the ground surface after it has been excavated and provides a firm and level base for the main concrete slab. Normally, the 100 to 150 mm (4 to 6 in) hardcore layer is 'blinded' with a 50 mm (2 in) layer of finer material (sand and fine gravel) which gives a smooth even surface on top of which is laid a *damp-proof membrane* (DPM) – typically heavy-duty (1000 gauge) polyethylene sheeting. This membrane is essential to prevent damp rising up through

the floor slab and it is tied in at the edges to the damp-proof course (DPC) in the walls, which prevents damp rising up through the brickwork. Sometimes, the DPM is laid under rather than over the floor slab.

The floor slab itself is 100 to 150 mm (4 to 6 in) thick and, in modern houses, a 50 mm (2 in) layer of expanded polystyrene is put between this and the cement screed to provide insulation. The screed is generally 50 mm (2 in) thick or 63 mm (2½ in) thick if the DPM is laid over the floor slab.

Older houses will not have any insulation and many will not have a damp-proof membrane – or, if they do have one, it may have failed.

SUSPENDED FLOORS

A 'suspended' timber floor consists of two parts: the *floor joists* running one way and the *floorboards* running the other.

The floor joists are supported by the outer walls of the house – and, for ground floors, by 'sleeper' walls – either by being put into holes left in the house walls or with joist hangers secured to the surface of the wall.

Timber *wallplates* are used on top of the sleeper walls, which must incorporate a damp-proof course (DPC). Joists used to support upper floors are larger than those used to support ground floors, because they have a longer unsupported span, and struts are generally fitted between the joists.

Timber floorboards are the traditional way of creating a suspended floor; in modern houses, they will often be replaced with sheets of flooring-grade chipboard (particle board). Both floorboards and chipboard sheets can have square edges or be 'tongued and grooved' – that is, a tongue on the side of one board (or sheet) fits into a groove on the edge of the neighbouring board or sheet. Tongued-and-grooved boards have the advantage that they fit together more securely without a gap for draughts; their disadvantage is that they are much more difficult to take up in the future.

The joists which support upper floors also provide support for the ceiling of the room below – typically sheets of plasterboard (dry wall or gypsum board) nailed to the underside of the joists.

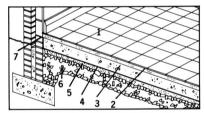

1 FLOOR COVERING
2 SCREED
3 FLOOR SLAB
4 DAMP-PROOF MEMBRANE
5 BLINDING LAYER
6 HARDCORE
7 DPC

SOLID FLOORS
The components of a solid floor, shown here with a tiled floor covering and in a house with cavity walls.

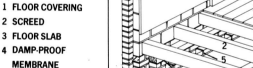

1 FLOORBOARDS
2 JOIST
3 DPC
4 WALLPLATE
5 SLEEPER WALL

SUSPENDED TIMBER FLOOR
A suspended timber ground floor, supported on 'honeycomb' dwarf walls.

COVERINGS FOR SUSPENDED TIMBER FLOORS
From the top: Plain narrow floorboard, tongued-and-grooved floorboard, plain wide floorboard, tongued-and-grooved flooring-grade chipboard (particle board).

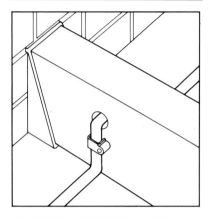

RUNNING CABLE UNDER FLOORS

Above: *The best place to run an electric cable is through a hole cut in the centre of a joist. If a notch has to be cut in the top of the joist, protect a cable (or a pipe) with a metal plate screwed over the top.*

UNDERFLOOR SERVICES

The space underneath floorboards or flooring sheets is used in houses to run essential services – electric cables, gas pipes, water pipes and central heating pipes. In a solid floor, similar services may be embedded in the concrete or laid inside a duct – and in some houses, special warming cables may have been installed in a solid floor to provide underfloor heating.

Because of the presence of electric cable or some kind of pipe below a timber floor surface, great care needs to be taken when drilling into the floor, putting in floorboard nails or using a saw to take up floorboards or floor sheeting. A simple metal detector can be used to determine the exact position of pipes and cables.

Underneath suspended ground floors, pipes and cables can be kept below the level of the joists, but underneath upper floor suspended floors, they must be run in the gap between the flooring and the ceiling underneath. Wherever possible, pipes and cables should be run parallel with the joists and clipped to them low down, so that they do not pose any threat to working on the floor from above. Where they have to be run across the joists (that is, parallel with the floorboards), electric cables should be run through holes cut in the centre of the joists, so that they are well away from floorboard nails or screws used to hold down flooring sheets. In a few instances, it may be possible to run water, gas and central heating pipes like this as well, but normally these will have to be fitted into notches cut out of the top of the joist. Ideally, a metal plate should then be fitted over the top of the pipe so that it is protected from nails or screws. In solid floors, pipes and cables should not be laid in direct contact with concrete and should be protected in some way.

For electric cables, the best answer is to bury a length of metal conduit in the floor screed and to run the cable inside that. For pipes, the ideal is to insert a purpose-made duct into the floor screed which has a removable cover so that access to the pipe (and especially joints in the pipe) is possible at a later date should a leak occur. The pipes themselves should be well insulated. In older houses, pipes may have been embedded directly into the concrete.

PIPES AND CABLES

Below left: *Underneath floorboards may lurk insulated central heating pipes and electric wiring cables. Note that pipes will normally be run in notches cut out of the top of the joists.*

Above: *A simple pipe and cable detector can tell you where services lie underneath a suspended timber floor.*

DIAGNOSING PROBLEMS

There is no point in laying a new floor covering of any kind on a faulty base, so the first thing to do is to have a good look at the floor and to assess whether it is in a good state of repair – or not.

SOLID FLOORS

The two main things you will be looking for here are unevenness (or breaking up) of the surface and damp.

Some floor coverings (such as cork or thin timber) demand a substrate that is absolutely flat. In these cases, an uneven solid floor, which might look fine if overlaid with less susceptible coverings, will have to be levelled in some way. If the floor is sound and basically dry, this is easily achieved using a floor levelling compound – see pages 26–27.

Slightly damp floors can also be dealt with, but if the floor is beginning to break up or shows signs of serious rising damp, it may be necessary to dig it up and re-lay it – a major undertaking. When dealing with a damp floor, you need to know whether the problem is rising damp or condensation – see page 26 for details.

TIMBER SUSPENDED FLOORS

A timber floor can be the victim of even more problems – the triple evils of damp, rot and woodworm. Before laying any floor covering, you should raise a few floorboards and have a good look around underneath with a torch, prodding any suspect areas with a sharp tool such as a small screwdriver or bradawl.

DAMP In timber floors, whether in the floorboards or the joists, damp is the beginning of all the problems and greatly increases the likelihood of rot and woodworm. For this reason, the walls surrounding suspended floors should contain airbricks to allow a free flow of air around the timbers to keep them dry. Some people block these up thinking that this will save money on heating costs or they may become blocked up accidentally. First, make sure that these airbricks are unclogged and that there are enough of them – there should be one single (brick-size) 225 by 75 mm (9 by 3 in) airbrick for every 1.2 m (4 ft) of wall.

WET ROT Water damage itself can be a serious problem leading to staining and wood decay, but an attack of rot is worse. Wet rot is the most common and can be identified by

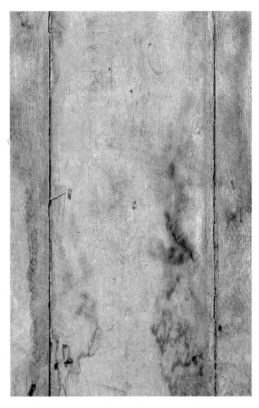

WATER DAMAGE
Left: *This is a typical example of water damage to the surface of floorboards – suspect the presence of rot underneath.*

WET ROT
Below: *Badly decayed and crumbling, these floorboards show the unmistakable signs of wet rot.*

a darkening, softening and splitting up of the timber, often with the timber cracking along the grain. A sharp tool can be pushed quite easily into affected areas. Fortunately, the damage is not difficult to repair once the rotten wood has been cut out, either by using a special hardener, followed by a filler for small attacks or by replacing the timber for more extensive outbreaks.

DRY ROT An attack of dry rot, however, is far more serious. This is characterized by grey/white strands on the surface of the timber, with the wood breaking into dry square-shaped pieces. In extreme cases, 'fruiting bodies' (a fungal growth) can form on the underside of the floorboards or the joists. The problem with dry rot (a misnomer since it happens only on damp timber) is that it can spread into, across and through masonry walls as well. The only solution is to remove – and burn – all affected timber (and plaster) and to replace it with new materials, treating all exposed surfaces with a special fungicide to prevent further attacks – a job probably best left to a professional remedial firm.

WOODWORM What is known generically as 'woodworm' is attack by one of a number of flying beetles, which lay their eggs in cracks and crevices in the timber. When the eggs hatch, the resulting larvae burrow into the wood and then stay there for anything up to four years, eating their way through and weakening the timber. Eventually they turn into flying beetles, burrow their way out of the wood and fly off to lay their eggs elsewhere. The clue to woodworm attack is the holes made by the beetles when they *leave*. These mean that you have had an attack not that they are still there. However, if you see these visible 'flight holes', the timber should be treated with a woodworm killer, particularly if there is fresh bore dust ('frass') on the surface indicating that a beetle has left recently. Treating small areas of attack can be done on a do-it-yourself basis, but large outbreaks should be left to a professional firm with the equipment (sprays and lances) necessary to reach all the areas which might be affected.

LOOSE AND BOUNCY FLOORING Before laying any new floor coverings on a suspended timber floor it is essential that you walk all over the floor to make sure there are no loose floorboards.

Jumping up and down on the floor – a 'bounce' test – will not only reveal loose floorboards but may also tell you about joists which have been weakened by attacks of rot or woodworm.

All these problems should be attended to as described on pages 16–19.

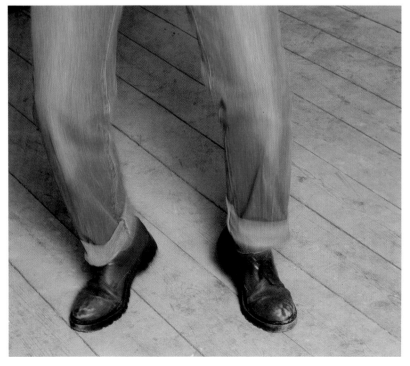

THE BOUNCE TEST

Before laying any new floor covering, make a series of bounce tests, flexing the floorboards to identify any that are loose and any weakened joists.

TOOLS AND EQUIPMENT FOR REPAIRING FLOORS

There are some specialist tools needed for repairing solid and suspended timber floors in addition to the general tools shown on pages 8 and 9.

1 Long spirit level Essential for checking both solid floors and suspended floors. Choose one at least 750 mm (2½ ft) long and if it is metal, it can double as a straight-edge for cutting.

2 Hammers Use a small cross-pein hammer (*top*) for nails and a claw hammer (*below*) for floor brads and for pulling nails, pins and brads out.

3 Floor brads These are the common 'cut' nails used for holding floorboards down. They force their way through the wood to hold it in place and are hammered flat to the surface.

4 Nails Ordinary nails can be used for fixing temporary floorboards or battens (furring strips).

5 Hand countersink This hand-operated tool is used for making the recess to take the head of a countersunk screw.

6 Carborundum block This can be used for smoothing down solid floors after floor levelling compound has been used.

7 Pipe and cable detector This can be used to determine the position of services running underneath a suspended timber floor.

8 Joist and batten detector Will register the position of flooring joists.

9 Steel float Also known as a plasterer's trowel, this can be used for spreading cement screeding and floor levelling compound out on a solid floor as well as for repairing damage to plastered walls.

10 Serrated float This is mainly used for spreading flooring adhesive leaving the adhesive in ridges to take floor coverings such as ceramic tiles.

11 Flooring trowel This trowel is larger than a plasterer's trowel and is ideal for spreading screed or floor levelling compound over a large area. It has a larger surface area than the plasterer's trowel and its pointed toe makes it easier to work right into corners.

12 Floorboard saw A specially designed saw for cutting across floorboards and along the gaps of tongued-and-grooved floor coverings to separate lengths.

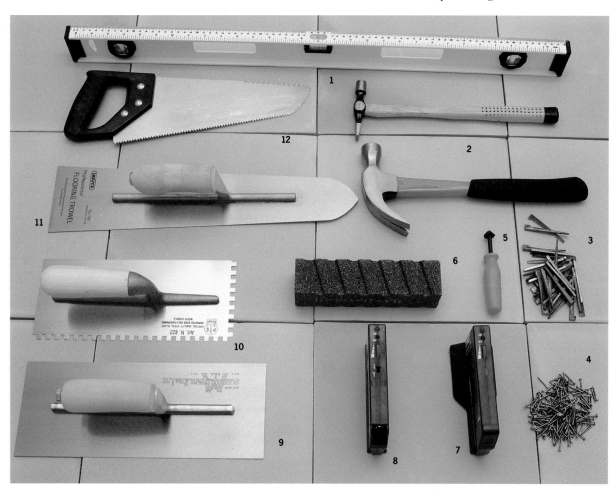

REPAIRING TIMBER FLOORS

Even if your timber floor does not have any of the more serious problems described on pages 13 and 14, there may still be minor problems which need to be solved before using the floor as a basis for a floor covering material or sanding it down and sealing it.

LOOSE FLOORBOARDS

By walking about on the floor, or by conducting a 'bounce' test (see page 14), you will soon discover which floorboards are loose and which are secure.

Loose floorboards are often the result of someone taking them up in the past and not putting them back properly or the nail holes having worn because they have been taken up and down several times.

Unless you know exactly where pipes and electric cables are underneath floorboards, it is always good practice to use the existing nail holes rather than attempting to put nails in new positions, which might be directly above a cable or pipe.

Sometimes, a loose floorboard can simply be secured by hammering the existing nail down into place (all protruding nails should be hammered down and punched just below the surface before using a floor sanding machine or before laying any type of floor covering). If the nail hole is obviously enlarged, a better answer is to remove the nail and put in a screw instead. Choose a size at least as long as the nail and of a diameter which will fill the nail hole – use a countersinking bit to make a recess for the screw head. Using an electric screwdriver will be much easier than putting the screws in by hand – especially if there are a lot to do.

REPLACING BOARDS

Sometimes a floorboard will have split or part of it will have broken off and the answer is to replace it – or at least part of it. If it is a short length already (perhaps cut out when new wiring was installed or central heating put in), you can replace the whole length; if it is only part of a board which is damaged, the existing board can be cut and only the damaged area replaced.

To cut through an existing floorboard, you should raise it from one end (in this case the damaged end) using a bolster (wide) chisel to lever it up and inserting wedges under the side until it has 'sprung' over the joist where you intend to cut it (perhaps leaving the nails behind). Then you can use a floorboard saw to cut through the floorboard exactly in the middle of a joist (which should be visible, or which can be found by sliding a thin-bladed knife along the gap at the edge of the board until it meets resistance). The floorboard saw has a curved edge so that you can saw through the board without damaging the boards on either side.

The new length of floorboard is then cut to the length of the gap and fitted in place with new nails or screws. First, check that the new board is the same width and thickness as the board it is replacing, planing it down to size first if necessary.

If the existing floorboard is tongued and grooved, you will need to cut along the gap on either side to remove the tongue before you do this. This can either be done with a floorboard saw or with a circular saw with the blade set to just less than the thickness of the floorboards.

Before using any kind of saw, it is essential to check first with a pipe and cable detector for the presence of electric cables and/or central heating pipes running below the floorboards.

REMOVING TONGUED-AND-GROOVED FLOORBOARDS

Above: *Use a floorboard saw to cut off the tongue of tongued-and-grooved floorboards before lifting them.*

REPLACING BOARDS

Right: *Use a punch to hammer floor brads below the surface of the floorboards. This is essential before laying a new floor covering or sanding down the floorboards.*

INSPECTION HATCHES

Even where the floorboards are sound and securely fixed, you may still want to remove a section to inspect the underfloor space or in order to put in a new light fitting in the room below. The answer is to cut through the floorboard at an angle using a jigsaw. This is done at the edge of a joist which is located with a thin-bladed knife as described in the section opposite, *Replacing Boards*. For tongued-and-grooved boards you can use a joist and batten (furring strip) detector or go by the position of the nails which should be centrally located on the joist. With the common 50 mm (2 in) joists, the edge should be roughly 25 mm (1 in) either side of the nail.

It is *vital* that you check for the presence of underfloor cables and/or pipes before cutting through a floorboard in this way.

In order to start the jigsaw cut, first drill a hole at the edge of the floorboard over the edge of the joist and then cut through the floorboard at a 45° angle – a jigsaw can be set to cut at this angle. Make a similar cut at the other end of the piece you want to remove unless the first cut is close enough to the end for the whole piece to be lifted out. Unless the piece is between two adjacent joists (where it can simply be lifted out), the first jigsaw cut should enable you to lever up the board (after cutting any side tongues off with tongued-and-grooved board).

Before replacing the board, cut a short length of 50 mm (2 in) square batten just wider than the floorboard and screw this to the side of the joist underneath. This then acts as a support for the length of floorboard removed – fit a second batten if you made a similar cut at the other end.

CUTTING AN INSPECTION HATCH

1 First drill through the edge of the floorboard next to a joist. This provides an access hole for the jigsaw blade.

2 Then use the jigsaw to cut through the board at an angle.

3 Lift or lever the old board out.

4 Before replacing the cut section of board, nail on a batten (furring strip) to the side of the joist to provide support.

GAPS IN FLOORS

In many older houses, you may find that your floorboards have significant gaps between them, which can allow a howling gale through if left unrepaired.

Large gaps can be filled by hammering in thin strips of wood shaped to the size of the gap and tapered slightly so that they 'wedge' into place – a good answer if you intend sanding the floor down and leaving it with the natural look. The strips are coated with woodworking adhesive and hammered into place, using a second piece of wood to protect the strip. Plane or sand down once the glue has dried.

One alternative is to use a flexible wood filler, but not the rigid filler used for repairing walls which would not cope with the natural movement of the floorboards as the humidity levels change. Another option is to use papier mâché. Made from strips of white paper and wallpaper paste, this is pushed into the gaps

and allowed to dry. In all these cases, the various filling materials can be stained afterwards to match the surrounding wood – or better still the whole floor can be stained to a uniform colour.

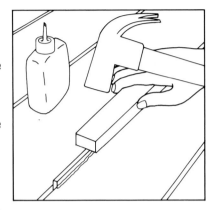

Hammer in thin strips of wood to fill gaps between floorboards.

NOISY FLOORBOARDS

To cure a noisy floorboard, replace the nails with screws. Make countersunk recesses for the screw heads first.

FILLING GAPS IN FLOORBOARDS

1 One method of filling between floorboards is to use a flexible wood filler.

2 Filler, repair strips and papier mâché take stain if your floorboards are to be left uncovered.

INSULATING SUSPENDED FLOORS

There are two reasons why you might want to insulate a suspended floor. With ground floors, it will be to stop heat escaping into the (cold) underfloor space; with upper floors, it will be to stop noise passing down through the floor.

Insulating floors is not easy as it involves taking up the whole floor covering, so this is something you would not normally consider doing unless replacing the floorboards anyway. There are two types of insulation material you can use – blanket or batts.

Insulating blanket is sold for use in lofts and can be used to insulate floors if netting (garden netting will do) is laid across the joists to provide a support for the insulation. Rigid insulation batts are sold mainly for insulating cavity walls but can be used for insulating floors if they are cut to the width between the joists and wedged into place.

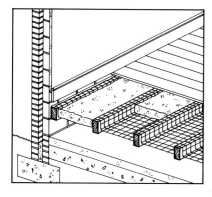

INSULATING FLOORS

To insulate a suspended floor, hang garden netting over the joists to support blanket insulation.

REPAIRS TO JOISTS

If joists have been overloaded or are too small for their span, they may have sagged causing the floor to become springy. This could also be caused by collapsed sleeper walls or by weakening of the joists (or the wallplates) as a result of rot or woodworm. In these cases, it may be necessary to replace or strengthen one or more joists.

To replace a whole joist will almost certainly mean lifting all the floorboards since cutting out sections of the boards above a single joist will be almost as much work. In any case, it is likely that if one whole joist needs replacing, others will, too. On upper floors, you will also need to remove part or all

of the ceiling below. The new joist can be put into the same joist hangers or holes in the wall as the old joist – when using holes, push the joist (cut to the correct length) as far as it will go into one hole, line up the end with the other hole and slide the joist back so it is resting on the wall in both holes (pack up with slate if necessary to bring the joist level with the other joists).

Sometimes only part of a joist will need replacing – where, for example, a section has rotted. Here, you cut out the damaged part of the old joist and bolt a new section on to the side of the old joist allowing a generous overlap. If it is the end of the joist which is being replaced, support the new section in a joist hanger.

Joists can similarly be strengthened by bolting a new section on to the side without cutting out any of the old joist.

If a joist has warped (twisted sideways), it might be possible to correct the warp by fitting new or additional 'herringbone' struts between the joists, first straightening the warp out with a car jack. The ends of the 50 × 25 mm (2 × 1 in) struts are angled to fit the joists and nailed in pairs between the joints at 1 m (3 ft) intervals. Drive the nails partway into the wood before putting the struts in position and nailing them down into the sides of the joist.

FITTING NEW FLOORBOARDS

Where a suspended timber floor has deteriorated badly, you might want to consider replacing all the floorboards – especially if you do not want to have any other floor covering. Otherwise, putting in sheet chipboard (particle board) flooring will be easier.

To fit new floorboards, the existing floorboards must first be removed, along with all the skirting boards (baseboards). Check the joists thoroughly for damage, strength and level – and repair, replace or strengthen as necessary. If insulation is being installed, do this before laying the new floorboards.

When laying new floorboards it is most important to get each board tight up against its neighbour. You can buy special flooring clamps to do this: these are attached to a joist and tightening the clamp forces the board up tight.

The floorboards should be cut to the length of the room less 20 mm (¾ in), with any shorter lengths cut so that the free end is centred on a joist. Fit the first board with its

NOISY FLOORBOARDS

Screwing down floorboards will stop most noises, which are caused by loose floorboards rubbing against one another or rubbing against the joists.

Another way of stopping floorboards squeaking is to dust talcum powder along the edges, but this will only serve as a temporary solution.

One possible cause of floorboards squeaking is that the joists have weakened allowing the floorboards to flex (something the 'bounce' test should show); this may call for more drastic measures to strengthen (or, in extreme cases, to replace) the joists – see *Repairing Joists*.

A noise from under the floorboards may also be caused by central heating pipes rubbing against the sides of a notch in the joists when they expand and contract as they heat up and cool down. The answer to this is to raise the floorboard over the offending pipe (it should be easy to identify this as it will have been lifted before to put the pipes in) and then to slip foam pipe insulation around the pipe where it crosses the joist, enlarging the notch if necessary. Under ground floors, insulate the whole pipe.

edge 10 mm (⅜ in) away from the wall and with its grooved edge (if using tongued-and-grooved boarding) facing the wall. Nail it in place with two nails into the centre of each joist, keeping well away from any pipes or cables laid in notches in the joists. Then lay the next five or six boards, using your floorboard clamp or wedges to force the whole group of boards up tight. To prevent damaging the tongue of the outside board, make the wedge which fits against it from a piece of the flooring so that it has a groove to go over the tongue. When you have wedged this group of boards, nail them all down and proceed with the next group.

Continue like this until you get to the far side of the room and plane or saw the last board down so that it fits into the gap with 10 mm (⅜ in) to spare (this gap and all the others will be covered by the skirting boards/baseboards when they are replaced). If the groove of the last board cannot be fitted over the tongue of the penultimate board, cut off the bottom edge of the groove so that it will drop into place.

REPAIRING CHIPBOARD (PARTICLE BOARD) FLOORS

Chipboard sheet flooring requires few repairs, unless it gets damp or if you need to make an inspection hatch for access to wiring or pipes. Because the large sheets are tongued and grooved, they are quite difficult (but not impossible) to remove once they are down.

You may also find that a chipboard floor can flex if additional timbers were not fitted between the joists to support the edges when the floor was first laid.

REMOVING CHIPBOARD (PARTICLE BOARD)

To remove a whole chipboard panel, you will first of all have to cut round all four edges to remove the tongues, using a circular saw set to just less than the thickness of the board, so that you do not damage the joists or any electric cables/pipes underneath. Then either undo the screws or punch home the nails before lifting the old board. Cut the tongues off the new board before re-laying it and fill the gap left with wood filler.

To cut out a section, find the location of the joists with a joist and batten (furring strip) detector (existing screws or nails will be a guide). Then use a circular saw to make two cuts alongside the edges of adjacent joists (or joists spaced two apart for a larger inspection hatch or more extensive damage), with two more cuts at right angles to square off the panel. Remove any screws (or punch home any nails) within the panel and lever it out. Before fitting a new section, screw support battens to the sides of the joists and, if possible, cross battens between the joists to support the edges. If any edges are left unsupported, screw battens to the underside of the chipboard surrounding the hatch (screwing through the chipboard into the batten) to provide adequate support for the cut-out section.

Where chipboard flooring might get damp in the future, seal the surface and all cut edges with PVA woodworking adhesive.

FITTING NEW CHIPBOARD (PARTICLE BOARD) FLOORING

Make sure that any chipboard you buy for flooring is *flooring grade*. This comes in two thicknesses – 19 mm (¾ in) and 22 mm (⅞ in); use 19 mm (¾ in) for joists spaced less than 450 mm (18 in) apart.

Both square-edge and tongued-and-grooved chipboard flooring is available. The advantages of tongued-and-grooved are that the edges meeting at right angles to the joists will support one another and that it will prevent draughts. On the other hand, it is more difficult to get up in the future.

Chipboard flooring is sold in large sheets 2.44 × 1.22 m (8 × 4 ft) and can be positioned on the floor so that the edges on the short side of a sheet meet in the centre of a joist. Smaller sheets are sold for boarding over lofts.

When using square-edge chipboard, fit 50 × 75 mm (2 × 3 in) supporting battens (furring strips) between the joists where the edges meet.

LAYING CHIPBOARD (PARTICLE BOARD) FLOORING

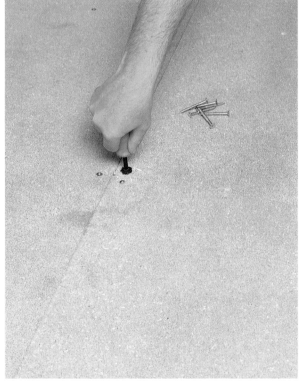

1 Chipboard sheet flooring is tongued and grooved on all edges so that one piece slots into the next.

2 The sheets are best held down with countersunk screws; drill a clearance hole in the chipboard first.

Start at one side of the room, leaving a gap of around 10 mm (⅜ in) between the wall and the grooved edge of the sheet (remove all skirtings/baseboards first). Screw the sheet to the joists, spacing the screws at about 300 mm (12 in) intervals and going into every joist. Drill clearance holes in the chipboard first and then make a countersunk recess – a cordless drill/screwdriver will make the whole job much easier. Position the second sheet so that the short edges do not line up and work around the room, finally cutting sheets to fit around the edges. Where there are pipe joints or electrical accessories below the floorboards, cut out an inspection hatch and fit supporting timbers below. For each board, use an off-cut of sheet with a groove along one edge plus a mallet to hammer home the sheet you have just laid. This will prevent any accidental damage.

To cut chipboard, use a circular saw fitted with a tungsten-carbide tipped (TCT) blade – ordinary blades will blunt quickly and handsaws even sooner.

LEVELLING FLOORS

If a wooden floor (floorboards or chipboard sheeting) is basically sound and dry, but is a little uneven, you can 'screed' it before fitting some kinds of floor covering (especially carpet, and thin sheet materials) in order to provide a smooth level surface.

The easiest material to use is hardboard sheeting laid rough side up. Like chipboard, this comes in large sheets, but it is relatively easy to cut with a sharp trimming knife and smaller sheets are available if required.

The hardboard sheeting should be left in the room where it is to be installed for a couple of days before putting it down (so that it takes up the temperature and humidity of the room). Nail it down to the floorboards using special hardboard nails around 150 mm (6 in) apart, making sure that the head of the nail is hammered flush with the hardboard surface. Remember to leave access panels where necessary.

As an alternative to hardboard, 6 mm (¼ in) plywood could be used, secured to the floorboards or chipboard floor with countersunk screws. Although a more expensive solution, this will give a more rigid result; on *very* uneven floors, hardboard will tend to take up the profile of the surface underneath over a period of time.

Where a floor is not level – as opposed to being uneven – it might be necessary to use the kind of floor levelling compound used on solid floors *after* covering the existing flooring with hardboard (see pages 26–27). This might be necessary when laying coverings such as woodstrip flooring or parquet in an older house where the foundations have sagged, giving a 'lean' to the floor, and might be a better bet than taking up the existing floor and re-laying it.

Coverings like carpet and vinyl do not need to be level (though they must be laid on a flat surface) and if you feel that a leaning floor gives 'character' to the house, it would be best to leave it that way, simply covering it with hardboard to get the necessary smooth, flat (but not level) surface.

LAYING PLYWOOD

Below: *Plywood screwed down to the existing flooring makes an ideal base for a new floor covering.*

LAYING HARDBOARD

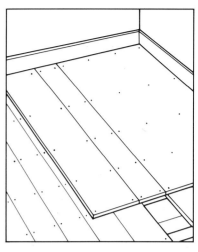

Above: *When laying hardboard sheeting, leave access panels for pipes and electrical accessories.*

REPAIRING STAIRS

If you are carpeting stairs there may be some repairs which need doing first. The three most common faults with stairs are creaking (caused by the supporting timbers working loose), worn 'nosings' — that is the front edge of each step losing its perfectly rounded shape — and loose balusters and handrails.

CURING STAIR CREAKS

Creaking stairs can be caused by a number of different faults.

A common cause is loose wedges. These are fitted on the underneath of the stair between the 'strings' of the stair (the two large pieces of wood up the side) and the individual 'risers' (vertical parts of the staircase) and 'treads' (horizontal components of the staircase). These wedges should be glued firmly in position, but they may have shrunk and the glue failed. Normally the solution is to remove the wedges, clean off the glue, apply new adhesive and hammer them back in position. Sometimes, the wedges may need reshaping to fit into position correctly.

Another cause can be loose or missing glue blocks which are fitted into the angle between each tread and riser on the underneath side of the staircase. To repair these simply clean off the old glue, apply new glue and replace the blocks. If they are missing, nail and glue quadrant moulding into place instead.

If there is still movement between a tread and a riser (which will cause a creak), there are two ways to prevent it. One is to put screws in from underneath, securing each tread to its corresponding riser. The other solution (useful where access to the underside of the stairs is limited) is to glue quadrant beading in from the top of the stair.

FIXING LOOSE WEDGES
Left: *Knock in wedges to cure creaking stairs; use a piece of wood to protect the wedge.*

REPLACING GLUE BLOCKS
Below: *If the glue blocks (shown at the top) are missing, glue and nail quadrant moulding in to secure the riser to the tread.*

SECURING TREADS TO RISERS

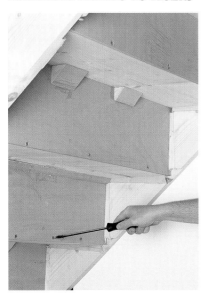

1 To secure a tread to a riser, put in screws from underneath.

2 Alternatively, if there is no access to the underside of the stairs, glue in quadrant beading from above.

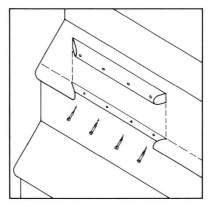

REPLACING NOSINGS

To repair a damaged nosing, cut out the damaged section carefully with a chisel and screw and glue in a new strip of moulding or a hand-shaped piece of timber. Alternatively, cut out and replace the whole strip.

CURING WORN NOSINGS

The rounded front edge of the stair receives a lot of punishment and is usually the first area to go. The answer is to cut out the worn section, fashion a new section from a suitable piece of timber and screw and glue it into place. It would be worth looking at the size and shape of rounded mouldings available from your local timber merchants/do-it-yourself store to see if any match the existing stair nosings. Hand shaping them from a solid piece of wood is time-consuming and requires a degree of skill.

If the treads of the stairs themselves have worn, giving a noticeably curved appearance, apply a flexible wood filler to these to make them flat again.

DEALING WITH WORN TREADS

Apply wood filler to worn treads to level the surface.

FIXING LOOSE BALUSTERS

LOOSE HANDRAILS AND BALUSTERS

Repairing loose handrails and balusters is ideally carried out at the same time as other remedial staircase repairs.

Small cracks in handrails can be cured by squeezing in a small amount of glue and clamping the two parts while the glue sets. Larger cracks or gaps may mean dismantling the stair rail and inserting dowels between the two halves, gluing and clamping the two parts together until the glue sets.

Loose balusters can usually be secured by hammering a nail at an angle in through the top of the baluster and into the handrail. To secure the bottom, insert a screw into the baluster through the side rail. If the baluster itself has split, a repair can usually be made with glue, clamping the two halves together (or holding them with tightly wound string) while the glue sets.

▲ **1** Secure the tops of loose balusters by 'skew' nailing into the handrail.

▼ **2** Secure the bottoms of balusters by inserting screws in the side rail.

REPAIRING SOLID FLOORS

Where you want to use a solid floor as a basis for a floor covering, ensure that it is sound, dry and level. Usually, it is possible to make repairs to a solid floor to bring it up to scratch; in extreme cases, it may be necessary to dig it up and lay a new floor.

REPAIRING THE SURFACE

Minor cracks in a solid floor can be ignored, but any large cracks or holes will need to be filled. This is a fairly simple task provided the floor is basically dry.

The crack or hole should be cleaned up and all loose material removed. If necessary, widen the crack to allow better penetration of the filler. To ensure good adhesion of the filler, prime the crack or the inside of the hole with a mixture of 1 part PVA adhesive/sealer and 5 parts water. Then mix up a mortar filler, consisting of 3 parts sand, 1 part cement (or use a quick-setting dry ready-mix mortar) and equal parts of PVA bonding agent and water. Apply the filler with a pointing trowel, pushing it well into the crack or hole. Deep holes may need filling in more than one layer; trowel over the top surface to smooth out the filling mortar.

Some solid floors suffer from 'dusting' – a tendency to be covered with a layer of dust which keeps on reappearing despite regular brushing. To prevent this cover the floor with a dilute solution of PVA adhesive/sealer or a special concrete sealer.

LOCAL REPAIRS TO SOLID FLOORS

1 First, line the sides of the hole with a mixture of mortar and PVA adhesive/sealer.

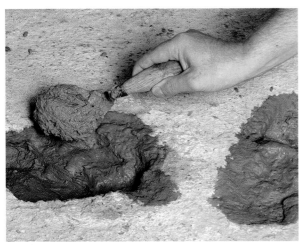

2 Then fill the hole with neat cement mortar.

3 Finally level off the surface with a plasterer's trowel.

LEVELLING A SOLID FLOOR

With some floor coverings, such as vinyl sheeting, it may not worry you that the floor undulates or slopes from one side to the other. But with other floor coverings, such as woodstrip flooring or many kinds of tiles, unevenness will be very noticeable once the covering is laid and the floor should be levelled before you start.

This is achieved with a special floor levelling compound which is spread out on the floor with a trowel to a maximum depth of

3 mm (⅛ in). Before you start, the floor should be thoroughly cleaned with a mixture of sugar soap and water and large holes and cracks filled with mortar and allowed to set; holes up to 5 mm (3⁄16 in) will be filled by the self-levelling compound.

The floor should be dampened before the levelling compound is laid and the compound itself mixed with water in a bucket until it forms a kind of slurry. Smooth it out as flat as possible with a trowel; it will level itself and the trowel marks will disappear. You can

normally walk on the floor after about two hours and the floor covering can be laid after about eight hours.

Skirting boards (baseboards) should be removed before floor levelling compound is used and replaced afterwards.

You may need to trim a small amount off doors which open into the room so they clear any new floor covering that has been laid over the newly levelled surface. Take these off before you start the job and check them before replacing.

DAMP-PROOFING A FLOOR

Dampness on a floor can be caused by one of two things – rising damp coming up from underneath or condensation, which is the result of warm moist air in the room meeting the cold floor surface. There is a simple test you can do to tell the difference, which is to invert a glass container on a ring of putty laid on the floor surface and leave it there for a couple of days. If water droplets collect on the *underside* of the glass container, the problem is rising damp; if they collect on the *outer* surface, the problem is condensation.

If the answer is rising damp and it is not too serious, the problem can be solved by painting or brushing two or more coats of a rubberized bitumen compound on the floor surface. This will act as a damp-proof membrane over which to lay your new floor covering. Remove the skirting boards (baseboards) and make sure that the bitumen compound is 'painted' up the walls as well as forming a continuous surface across the floor. A more serious rising damp problem indicates that there is no existing damp-proof membrane further down (common with older 'brick-on-earth' floors) and the only real answer is to dig the floor up and start again – a major undertaking.

If the problem is condensation, it would still be a good idea to use a rubberized bitumen compound, but you should also use a floor covering which has some insulation properties (such as cushioned vinyl or floor coverings containing cork). These will make the surface warmer than, say, using quarry tiles. At the same time take other measures to reduce the amount of moisture in the air such as fitting extractor fans in kitchens.

CONDENSATION OR DAMP?
An upturned glass container on a ring of putty reveals whether a damp floor problem is caused by rising damp or condensation.

USING FLOOR LEVELLING COMPOUND

1 Before putting down floor levelling compound, give the whole floor a coating of diluted PVA adhesive/sealer.

2 After mixing up, simply pour the floor levelling compound out over the floor.

3 A flooring trowel is ideal for spreading levelling compound reasonably flat.

4 The compound should level itself, but rub down any bumps with a carborundum block.

DECORATING DECISIONS

The floor and its floor covering is one of the most important elements of any room. It determines its sound and its feel, its texture and pattern can set the key for the room's style and, on a practical level, it is the surface on which you walk and on which furniture is placed.

There are many factors which need to be taken into account when choosing a floor covering, both practical points and aesthetic considerations.

There is nothing to beat the lovely mellow aged look inherent in terracotta tiles. Warmer underfoot than quarry or ceramic tiles, they soon take on a deep patina.

CHOICES

There is no point having a luxury carpet if it is going to be ground down by excessive wear (the main wear point on carpets is where people change direction, such as the bottom of stairs or corners in a corridor) or a fine polished floor in the hall which gets scratched to bits by people walking in from the garden. Equally, you will want a covering in kitchens and bathrooms which can resist water. You will also want to think about how the floor covering *sounds* – some hard floor coverings can be very noisy – and *feels*, especially if you like to walk around barefoot. Ask yourself:

- what will the room be used for?
- will the floor covering be subject to heavy wear?
- will people walk on the floor covering directly after being outside?
- is the floor likely to get wet?
- does the floor need to match existing furniture and decorations?
- do you have underfloor heating (electric cables buried in a solid floor)?
- are there any problems with the existing floor (especially if the new floor covering is heavy)?
- do you need access to underfloor services (plumbing and electrics)?
- how much will it cost?

Floor coverings divide neatly into two groups – *hard* floors (such as brick, ceramic and quarry tile and timber) and *soft* floors (such as carpet, lino, vinyl, rubber and cork). All floor coverings need a sub-floor to rest on, except thick woodstrip flooring which can be used to replace floorboards.

HARD FLOOR COVERINGS

BRICK floors can look 'rural' and, depending on the colour of bricks chosen, warm. Bricks are less cold underfoot and less noisy than ceramic or quarry tiles, and are generally waterproof and non-slip. They are moderately expensive and suitable only for solid ground floors and should be laid on a bed of mortar over a damp-proof membrane. Make sure that *paving* bricks are used.

CERAMIC tiles used for flooring are thicker than the type familiar for use on walls. A wide variety of sizes, shapes and patterns is available in both machine-made and hand-made versions. Ceramic floor tiles are laid on a bed of adhesive either on a solid floor or on a suspended timber floor, strengthened with exterior-grade plywood. The tiles are extremely durable and are easy to keep clean, although they are expensive, cold underfoot and noisy; some have a surface texture to make them non-slip.

QUARRY tiles, usually square or rectangular, are also popular and come in the same range of warm colours as bricks. They are very durable and can be a relatively cheap way of covering a floor but, like ceramic tiles, are cold and noisy underfoot (though less likely to crack than ceramic). Machine-made quarry tiles of even thickness are laid on adhesive; hand-made quarries are laid on a cement mortar screed.

TERRACOTTA tiles are similar to quarry tiles but are warmer underfoot and, because they are porous, need to be sealed.

STONE, MARBLE, SLATE AND TERRAZZO (originally chips of marble set in concrete and ground smooth) all have their advantages and their own appeal, but are expensive and usually need to be laid professionally.

WOODSTRIP flooring (usually hardwood) gives the appearance of floorboards, but without the gaps. Thin types are laid on top of an existing floor; thick types can replace floorboards.

WOOD MOSAIC flooring consisting of tiny strips of wood held on to a backing to give larger panels.

WOODBLOCK 'parquet' flooring is made up of small blocks of wood, usually laid in a herringbone pattern.

All these wood floorings will give a fine attractive covering to a solid or suspended timber floor; wood mosaic is the cheapest and easiest to lay; woodblock parquet flooring the most expensive and the most difficult to put down.

In order to resist wear and water, timber flooring needs to be sealed, unless it comes pre-sealed. It is fairly warm underfoot and durable (if properly sealed), but can be noisy to walk on.

Although not easy to lay, slate tiles are a traditional flooring material. These tiles are of Indian slate; note the charming irregularity in the natural colours.

SOFT FLOOR COVERINGS

CARPETING is the most familiar type of soft floor covering, available in several different types and qualities (and prices). Special types of carpet are available for use in kitchens and bathrooms, where they need to be water resistant, and in other rooms you will want to choose a carpet with a wear characteristic suitable to the room's use. However, foam-backed carpet should never be used with underfloor heating.

CARPET TILES are an inexpensive and easy way of covering floors and have the advantage that the individual tiles can be taken up for cleaning or can be replaced when they wear.

Right: Carpet tiles can provide an ideal flooring material for bathrooms. Here two contrasting colours have been used .

Cork tiles provide a warm, quiet and resilient floor covering which is extremely durable. Here, two layers of cork have been used – a facing veneer layer and a backing layer – and the whole tile is sealed with a vinyl coating.

VINYL, available in both sheet and tile form, comes in a huge range of colours and patterns and in both plain and cushioned versions. Warm and quiet underfoot and resistant to water, oil, fat and most chemicals found in the home, vinyls are relatively inexpensive and are ideal for use in kitchens, bathrooms and children's rooms; the sophisticated range of patterns now available also makes them a good choice for halls and dining rooms. They will not, however, stand up to burns nor to abrasion from grit. Vinyl is usually stuck down to the surface with adhesive; tiles are easier to lay (and less likely to shrink) than sheets. Wear can be improved by using a special vinyl floor polish.

LINO (linoleum) is increasing in popularity after years of decline. Available in sheet and tile form, it is made from natural materials. It has many of the advantages of vinyl, but is more durable, more expensive and more difficult to lay. Lino tiles can be laid like vinyl tiles, but laying sheet lino is a job best left to professionals.

CORK floor tiles provide a really warm floor surface. This flooring is relatively inexpensive, warm, quiet, resilient and surprisingly hardwearing, provided it is well sealed and laid on a flat surface. It is held down with adhesive (many tiles are self-adhesive) and is easy to cut. Cork should not be used with underfloor heating.

RUBBER flooring, familiar in offices and shops but now increasingly used in the home, is also available in tile form. Warm and quiet underfoot, this flooring is not cheap, but is extremely durable, water resistant and easy to clean.

COIR, SISAL AND SEAGRASS mattings provide an inexpensive floor covering, and are hardwearing and easy to lay. For laying from wall to wall, sew pieces together and bind the edges with jute tape.

Right: Sisal is a natural hardwearing floor covering material and is easy to keep clean. It can be used as individual rugs as shown here (with jute edging tape) or can be fitted from wall to wall.

RUGS A single floor covering can often be bland (as with plain carpet) or too harsh on the ear and the eye (quarry tiles and timber flooring) and many people will want to consider using rugs and mats.

There is an enormous variety available to suit every taste and every pocket. Apart from adding colour and pattern, rugs can also be used to define particular areas – a rug surrounded by chairs and a sofa could delineate a seating area, for example.

Just a selection of some of the highly coloured Indian rugs available, hand-made from natural materials.

ROOM BY ROOM FLOOR COVERINGS

Although in theory you can use virtually every type of floor covering in every room, some types are better suited than others, either from a practical point of view or for appearance's sake. Bear the following points in mind before making your choice.

LIVING ROOMS You will obviously want living-room floor coverings to look good, but wear is a primary consideration. Coir and sisal matting are both attractive and hardwearing choices, but the best choice for a soft floor covering is probably a 80/20 per cent wool/nylon carpet (or 100 per cent wool if you can afford it).

Hard floor coverings can be particularly effective in living rooms. Choose either wood or cork, with a few rugs scattered around (on non-slip underlay). If the existing floorboards are sound, sand them down and seal them with floor varnish, perhaps painting or stencilling them first.

DINING ROOMS As food and liquid are likely to get spilt in a dining room, practicality is as important as comfort and good looks. If you want carpet, you must be prepared to clean it regularly, but good choices for dining rooms are vinyl, lino or sealed cork – or a timber floor covered with rugs (on non-slip underlay). Ceramic tiles will look good (and be easy to keep clean) but will be noisy – especially as chairs are dragged across them.

HALLS As the hall is often the first part of your home that visitors see, you will want a floor covering which looks good. Carpet will need to be good quality to withstand the likely wear (particularly if the hall leads directly from the street or the garden); hard tiles or wood flooring will be easier to keep clean. In an older house, hard tiles were the traditional floor covering in a hallway – an effect which can be achieved now by using patterned vinyl or lino.

BEDROOMS Softness underfoot is the most important thing here and the usual choice will be carpet fitted from one wall to the other. In a child's or baby's room, consider using vinyl, lino or sealed cork which provide a hardwearing and easy-to-clean surface. If you prefer wood flooring, use plenty of rugs to stand on, but make sure they cannot slide around by putting them on a non-slip underlay.

Above: *Natural floorboards can look really good in a living room if sanded and sealed, and can provide the perfect backdrop for wood and cane furniture, varnished skirtings (baseboards) and colourful rugs.*

Left: *A woodstrip floor is easy to keep clean in a busy hallway and provides a warm, welcoming approach as well as reflecting some of the available light.*

STAIRS Durability is very important on stairs. The best choice is a hardwearing carpet, but avoid long piles (especially shag pile) in which high heels could get caught.

BATHROOMS Most floor coverings can be used in bathrooms, but avoid ceramic tiles which can be slippery when wet. Special carpets are sold for use in bathrooms; avoid the wool types which can rot. Vinyl, lino and sealed cork are ideal.

KITCHENS Practicality is the most important thing here and your choice may well depend on the existing sub-floor. Solid floors can be covered with virtually any floor covering, while suspended wooden floors may not be strong or stable enough for ceramic or quarry tiles. Vinyl, rubber and sealed cork are all ideal for kitchens; quarry tiles and ceramic tiles are easy to keep clean, but are cold and noisy underfoot. If you use carpet, make sure it is a type suitable for kitchens.

CONSERVATORIES The type of floor covering you choose for a conservatory will depend very much on how the conservatory is to be used. For traditional plant displays, a hard easy-to-clean covering, such as ceramic, terracotta or quarry tiles, will be best; if the conservatory is an extension of the living space, you might want to continue your existing flooring (timber or carpet, say) into the conservatory.

Above left: *The natural yellow and beige appearance of seagrass is at home almost anywhere in the house. Its hard, almost impermeable, fibre makes it an ideal choice for the tough job of covering stairs.*

Above: *Vinyl tiles are an ideal floor covering for bathrooms and today's designs are extremely stylish.*
Below: *Terracotta floor tiles make for a beautiful kitchen floor.*

DESIGN CONSIDERATIONS

Since the floor makes up one of the largest single areas of any room to be furnished and decorated, its colouring, pattern and design need to be chosen very carefully for the overall scheme to be a success.

Because flooring materials must be hardwearing as well as decorative, they tend to be expensive, especially in the large quantities required, and are therefore replaced less frequently than other furnishings. Costly mistakes will have to be lived with for a long time; it also makes sense to choose a colour and style that will suit various schemes so that you will not be restricted to the same style of paint, paper and fabric until you can justify replacing the flooring.

First, you must consider which types of floor covering are most suitable before narrowing your choice down to colour and pattern. For each of the flooring types, think about things like its durability, comfort, ease of laying (if you plan to do the job yourself) and cost, using the information provided in this chapter and in the rest of the book.

When thinking about colour and pattern, look at surface texture as well. This can make such a difference to your choice of other furnishings. Too many thick velvety surfaces, for example, can be a little oppressive; a room with a hard shiny floor with lots of gloss paint, mirrors and, maybe, ceramic tiles on the walls is not very relaxing. A variety of contrasting textures between flooring and other furnishings usually makes a more comfortable impression, although you may wish to use a certain type of flooring to create a special effect or style statement.

For example, a hard shiny surface in the living area creates a sense of smartness and slickness, while carpet in the bathroom provides an unmistakable sense of luxury.

Below: A light and airy country-style room is perfectly offset by the real brick hearth and the natural effect of timber floorboards.

Left: *Carpet can provide a luxurious feel to a bathroom. Here, a woven Axminster carpet made of 80 per cent wool and 20 per cent nylon has been used.*

VISUAL EFFECTS

You can create optical illusions with your choice of colour and pattern: strong, dark colours will make a room appear smaller and the ceiling lower, while a light, neutral all-over design such as a plain or lightly flecked carpet, cork, coir or timber can be used to create the impression of space. Laying a strong pattern on the diagonal will also give the impression that the room is rather larger than it is.

Decorative borders (perhaps with lino flooring – see page 89) are helpful for defining an area and also to create a strong decorative theme. An infinite number of original designs is possible, especially using the different shapes and colours available among ceramic and quarry tiles or woodblock flooring.

Few classic designs are more striking than the traditional two-coloured chequerboard effect of alternating black (or similarly dark-coloured) tiles with white. With ceramic, stone, vinyl and lino tiles you can use octagonal white squares with small black squares (insets) to fill in the gaps.

Right: *A bold coordinated design in strong colours is achieved here by painting natural floorboards to contrast with the walls, the furniture and the soft furnishings.*

Ceramic, lino and vinyl tiles all offer a wonderful variety of colours and motifs, but subtler, equally stunning, effects can be created using different shapes or configurations. Bricks and woodblocks can be laid in basketweave or herringbone patterns as well as the more familiar 'bonded' pattern; interlocking parquet or quarry tiles can be used to make up your own design.

However, this bold kind of treatment is not to everyone's taste. A patterned floor can make the rest of the room difficult to coordinate, unless the pattern is tiny or unobtrusive. A plain colour or flecked effect makes it easier to choose the rest of the room's furnishings; if you are worried it is looking too dull, a more neutral flooring can be livened up with rugs, mats or furniture.

If you are hoping to match the colour of your carpet or other floor covering exactly to certain other furnishings, then you should cut a tuft or snippet from a place where it will not be noticed or from an off-cut or sample of the material and take it with you to compare when you buy the floor covering.

Colours can be very tricky to match correctly from memory and you may find it easier if you opt instead for a paler or darker shade of the same hue or even a complementary or contrasting colour – red or pink, for example, can look very good against grey, while yellow is the traditional companion for green.

Remember that light can change colours dramatically so think about how and when the room is most likely to be used. Enhance a room receiving the late afternoon sunshine with honey shades of gold, brown and russet. Avoid blues and cold greens in a north-facing room or one with little natural light to prevent a chilly effect, especially where there are a lot of shiny surfaces, such as in a bathroom. If the room will be mainly used in artificial light, do check under a lamp with your samples: some reds and greens go brown, while blue might look black or grey. The secret is to beg, borrow or buy a sample of tile, carpet or whatever your choice of flooring and live with it *in situ* for a few days. You will soon see if it suits.

Above left: *This Axminster woven carpet recreates traditional designs from the primitive and isolated Feraghan district of Persia. Available with a matching border, the 80 per cent wool and 20 per cent nylon woven carpet is suitable for all parts of the home.*

Above right: *Just one of the enormous range of elegant patterns obtainable with woven Axminster carpets. Using a mixture of wool and nylon for maximum comfort and durability, the carpets are just as much at home in the bathroom as in the living room.*

DESIGNING WITH WALL TILES

The endless variety of sizes and patterns of wall tiles mean that you can be very imaginative in their use.

You will want to choose a colour of tile which matches the overall colour scheme, but while a small bathroom may be suited to tiles in just one colour, there is no reason why different tiles should not be used over a basin to contrast with the sanitary ware colour or on a windowsill to coordinate with the curtain material.

If you use different colours of tiles in your overall design, these can be mixed like the squares on a chequerboard or as chevrons, while single tiles of one expensive pattern can be interposed at random in among tiles of another cheaper pattern; or a line of the second pattern can be placed above the skirting (baseboard), worktop or bath; below a ceiling, horizontally along a wall at dado (chair) rail height or around a fireplace.

Smaller border tiles can be used to define the area of tiling or to create panels within the tiled area, perhaps around pictures or mirrors. Rounded edge tiles could equally be used for contrast. If you want to change the pattern on existing tiles, you can buy tile transfers which are simply stuck to the surface – either on all the tiles or just on selected ones.

Above right: *Narrow border tiles produce a 'picture frame' around this bathroom basin, while random feature tiles combine well with the plant display.*

Right: *The clever use of contrasting patterns of tile, plus border tiles and random feature tiles produces a dramatic effect in this country-style kitchen.*

Below: *A charming combination of plain white ceramic tiles with traditional 'Delft' pottery baskets.*

WOOD FLOORS

Wood has many advantages as a flooring material. It is relatively warm underfoot; it is less noisy than ceramic or quarry tiles (though, of course, not as quiet as a 'soft' flooring); it provides good insulation if there are no gaps; and, above all, it has its own beauty as a natural material. Wood floors *can* be painted, but the majority are left with a natural finish, sometimes enhanced by a wood stain and usually covered with a protective coat of varnish or floor sealer.

The golden colour of this woodstrip flooring echoes beautifully the natural pine door, door surround and timber mouldings.

OPTIONS

There are three ways you can have a new wood floor. One is to restore existing floorboards by sanding them down to a new finish; another is to replace existing floorboards with new floorboards or thick woodstrip flooring; the third is to lay a timber floor covering down over the existing floor, whether this is a suspended timber floor or a solid concrete floor.

RESTORING EXISTING FLOORBOARDS

If the existing floorboards are not damp, have no signs of rot and are basically in good structural condition, you can simply grind off the surface dirt, grime and irregularities with a floor sander and get back to a reasonably good finish. This can then be stained and varnished after any remaining minor faults have been repaired. See pages 16–19 for details of this.

NEW FLOORBOARDS

If an existing suspended timber floor is in a poor state of repair, it may not be possible to restore the existing floor. In this case new floorboards are the only answer if you want to keep the same type of flooring.

Note that floorboards are made from softwood, which marks easily and is pale white in colour, so they may need some kind of wood stain to enhance their looks if you are leaving the floor bare. Note, too, that floorboards may have faults (knots, splits, cracks, warps or bows) when you buy them – and that these faults can also develop over a period of time.

Laying new floorboards is covered in detail on page 19; the alternative is thick woodstrip flooring as described below.

TIMBER FLOOR COVERINGS

There are three main types of timber floor covering available: strip, mosaic and block.

STRIP FLOORING is sold either as individual planks (like floorboards) or in larger sheets with individual strips joined together to look like floorboards. The planks or the sheets are tongued and grooved so can be laid down on the floor with no gaps.

Woodstrip flooring comes in different thicknesses – typically 8 to 9 mm (⅜ in), 12 to 15 mm (½ in), 19 mm (¾ in) and 23 to 25 mm (1 in). The thinner types are designed to be laid directly on to an existing floor; the

thicker types are also suitable for securing to joists in place of floorboards or chipboard (particle board) flooring. Most woodstrip flooring is hardwood (oak, beech, elm, merbau or teak), though softwood (pine) is also available. The thicker woodstrips usually have a thin top layer of hardwood laminated to two sub-layers of softwood. The widths of woodstrip flooring vary from 125 mm (5 in) to 200 mm (8 in) and more; lengths are typically 1.8 m (6 ft) and 2.4 m (8 ft).

The advantages of hardwood strip floorings over softwood floorboards are that they are more durable, more resistant to marking and more colourful – hardwoods generally are much more attractive than softwoods. Because of the way hardwood strip flooring is constructed, there should also be no faults in the material and it should be completely stable, neither warping, bowing nor splitting.

Woodstrip flooring can be secured with nails into the timber floor or joists below or with adhesive or clips to join adjacent strips together to give a 'floating' floor.

MOSAIC FLOORING consists of narrow strips of wood, attached to a hessian (burlap) backing or joined together with wire and glue in squares, so that the strips in one square are at right angles to the strips in the adjoining squares. A 'panel' is usually four squares.

Mosaic panels vary in size from 300 mm (12 in) square to 600 mm (24 in) square with a

thickness of between 7.5 mm (⁵⁄₁₆ in) and 10 mm (⅜ in). The method of construction allows a degree of flexibility so the flooring can cope with slightly uneven surfaces.

Mosaic flooring comes in a choice of different woods (merbau, oak, iroko and pine, for example) and either has a self-adhesive backing or is laid on a bed of adhesive. Each panel is usually tongued and grooved.

BLOCK FLOORING consists of small blocks of wood which are laid down individually in a pattern, of which by far the most common is 'herringbone'. This type of flooring is often known as *parquet*, though 'parquet' is commonly used to describe other types of timber flooring as well.

Parquet flooring blocks can vary in thickness from 6 mm (¼ in) to 50 mm (2 in) and individual blocks are typically 225 to 300 mm (9 to 12 in) long and 50 to 75 mm (2 to 3 in) wide. The blocks are laid on a bed of mastic or asphalt on the sub-floor (commonly a concrete floor), but laying parquet requires skill and is a job for a professional.

Another type of timber flooring consists of a thin layer of hardwood on a cork base with a protection of vinyl. This not only looks good but is warm. It is laid on adhesive in a similar way to cork floor tiles – see page 88.

Natural wood floorboards can be acoustically perfect for musicians, as well as an attractive complement to wood furniture.

TYPES OF WOOD FLOORING

1 Tongued-and-grooved woodstrip flooring; *left to right* darkened beech, white pigmented beech, ash, natural beech, and oak.

2 Mosaic panel.

3 Woodstrip flooring specifically designed to imitate traditional parquet flooring.

The other examples show the vast range of woodstrip flooring available.

FLOORING EQUIPMENT

1 Floor sander The large machine on the left is a drum floor sander which you can hire from a local hire shop. The hire shop will also sell the **sanding sheets** (2) it needs in fine, medium and coarse grades, which are fitted around the drum.

3 Edging sander A drum floor sander cannot get right into the edges of the floor, so for this you need an edging sander (also available for hire) plus **sanding discs** (4).

5 Disc sander A useful tool for sanding around obstructions, such as door mouldings and pipes passing through the floor, and for sanding right into corners. Use with care to avoid damage.

6 Hammers You will need one or more hammers – for punching down existing floorboard nails, for 'secret nailing' of strip flooring and for forcing strips and sheets of flooring up against one another.

7 Paint brushes For applying wood stain, varnish and sealer. Choose two sizes – the large one for the main body of the floor; a smaller one for the edges and for getting round obstacles.

Some general tools you will need for laying timber flooring include saws, planes, chisels, nail punches, tape measure, try square, pencil and trimming knife.

SANDING FLOORS

You can sand down any old wooden floor – woodblock, mosaic woodstrip or floorboards – but it is almost certain that if you hire a sanding machine you will be working on floorboards, which may have curled at the edges and suffered considerable surface damage after years of use.

PREPARING THE FLOOR

The first thing to do is to empty the room of all furniture and remove any rugs, carpet or other floor coverings. Bear in mind that sanding the floor will create a lot of dust, so take anything else out of the room (such as books on shelves) which you do not want to get covered in dust. Alternatively, you can cover them with a dust sheet sealed at the edges. It is a good idea when sanding to remove the door into the room (so you can get at the floor beneath it), but to seal the door opening with a large plastic sheet taped around the opening on the far side and then to open windows in the room to allow dust to escape while you work.

The first thing to do is to look at the existing floorboards for damp, rot and woodworm as described on pages 13–14, preferably taking up a couple of boards to inspect the joists as well. Carry out a 'bounce' test (see page 14) to make sure the floor is firm. Carry out any remedial treatment and replace any split or damaged floorboards with new ones of the same size.

Now look at the existing floorboard nails. You should be able to see or feel any which are protruding and these should be hammered home below the surface with a nail punch. Where tacks are left in the floor from previous floor coverings, use an old chisel to lever the tacks up and then use a pair of pliers, pinchers or a claw hammer to pull them out. Nails and tacks left in place will damage the sanding belts.

Fill any gaps between floorboards as described on page 18. If the floor is to be varnished afterwards, mix some sawdust with the filler to fill small gaps (or use a coloured filler) so that it blends in with the rest of the flooring.

It is a good idea to remove old floor polish before sanding or it can clog the sanding belt. Use wire wool dipped in white (mineral) spirit to do this. If the floor has been painted, remove at least some of the paint with paint stripper and a scraper first, followed by water or white spirit (depending on the type of paint stripper used). Allow a couple of days for the floor to dry out before using a sanding machine.

PROTECTIVE CLOTHING

Because sanding produces a lot of dust, you should wear a face mask and, preferably, well-fitting eye protectors. You will also need ear muffs as floor sanders make a lot of noise – and choose a time for sanding when it will not upset your neighbours. Avoid wearing loose flapping clothing.

PREPARATION

1 Your old floor may look like this, with layers of old floor wax, splashes of paint and rusty nail heads above the surface.

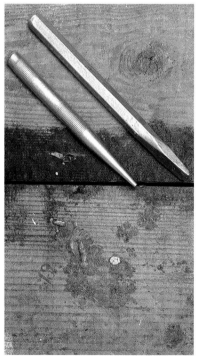

2 Punch floorboard nails below the surface – and, if required, fill the hole.

3 To remove old flooring tacks, use an *old* chisel to lever the nail up and then pull it out with pliers, pincers or the claw of a claw hammer.

USING THE FLOOR SANDER

Before you start, fit a new belt to the sanding machine. Instructions will be provided on how to do this, but normally you have to loosen the screws on the gripper bar so that you can secure the two ends of the sanding sheet under it, passing a single sheet around the drum. With many floors, you will be able to start with a medium-grade sheet, but if the floorboards are curled up at the edges, start with a coarse sheet.

When using a floor sander, make sure that the cable of the machine is safely out of the way over your shoulder and always hold the machine firmly with both hands. Tilt it backwards before you start it and then lower it gently on to the floor. It will try to run away from you, but hold it firmly and walk across the floor with it. When you get to the other side of the room, tilt the machine up again to turn it round.

With curling floorboards, use the sander diagonally across the room, starting in one corner and working across to the opposite corner, going back and forth over each area several times. Then repeat the process sanding diagonally the other way.

When you have levelled out any curled floorboards, change the belt for a medium grade and work up and down the floor parallel with the floorboards. This is where you would start with a floor which was not too badly damaged or when sanding woodstrip or mosaic flooring (which should only ever be sanded lightly); herringbone-pattern parquet block flooring should be sanded diagonally in line with the individual strips. When you have covered the room with the medium-grade belt – and are satisfied that no areas of floor have been missed – switch to the fine belt and go up and down the floor, again parallel with the floorboards.

You will now be left with a strip all around the edge of the room which is unsanded. Use the edge sander for this, starting with medium-grade disc and finishing with fine (you should not need coarse).

Finally sweep or vacuum up all the dust from the floor and go over it with a dry lint-free rag to remove any residual particles.

Above: *A sanded floor provides a perfect setting for furniture, rugs and soft furnishings and, if varnished, will help reflect the light.*

SANDING PROCEDURE

1 To change the sanding belt on a floor sander, tip the machine on its side and use a screwdriver to release the gripper bar.

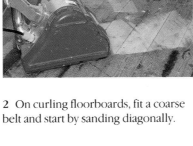

2 On curling floorboards, fit a coarse belt and start by sanding diagonally.

3 Keep working diagonally across the floor until you have covered it and then repeat going diagonally the other way.

4 Then fit a medium belt and sand up and down the floor parallel with the floorboards. Repeat with a fine-grade belt.

5 Finish off by going along the skirtings (baseboards) with an edge sander and using a disc sander in the corners.

LAYING TIMBER FLOORING

Whether laying wood mosaic flooring or strip flooring, the first job is to prepare the floor as described on pages 10–27. Solid floors may need damp-proofing and the application of a self-levelling compound; suspended timber floors will need to be made good and then covered with hardboard or plywood sheets to make them flat. New concrete floors should be left for a couple of months to dry out thoroughly before a floor covering is laid.

You will get a better result if you remove the skirtings (baseboards) before laying timber flooring – but you may damage them in the process which will mean replacement (and redecoration).

MEASURING UP

You will need to measure up the size of the floor you need to cover. Timber floor coverings (especially hardwood strip flooring) are expensive and you do not want to buy more than you have to.

Before measuring up, check the size of the timber flooring of your choice and check how it is sold, so that you can estimate exactly how many strips or how many packs to buy.

To calculate how much you will need, draw an accurate plan of the room (a scale of 1:20 is about right), measuring the width and length of the room at several points. Remember that floorboards and thick woodstrip flooring are laid at right angles to the joists, while thin woodstrip flooring is laid at right angles to existing floorboards. For mosaic and some woodstrip flooring, work out the *area* to be covered as packs will usually be quoted in areas.

With all types of flooring, allow around 5 per cent extra for cutting and wastage and for future repairs.

Before laying any timber flooring, unwrap the panels from their packaging and leave them in the room where they are to be laid for a couple of days so that they take up the room's moisture content – this prevents expansion or contraction later.

LAYING WOOD MOSAIC FLOORING

When buying mosaic panels, check to make sure that they are all the same size. Any slight variation will leave unsightly gaps in the finished floor.

Before laying mosaic panels in earnest, line up a row of panels without adhesive along the length of the room to check positioning. Remembering to leave a gap of 12.5 mm (½ in) at the edge (for expansion), try to arrange the flooring so that the first and last panels are approximately the same size. Also make sure that any cutting is done up the sides of 'fingers' rather than across the middle of a 'finger'. If the panels are hessian (burlap) backed, this is easily done using a trimming knife. With a wired panel, simply cut through the wire with a hacksaw and break the glue joint. If 'fingers' do need to be cut through, hold the panel firmly in a vice and cut through the 'finger' carefully with a tenon saw (backsaw).

When you are happy with the position of the panels, remove them all except the central one and mark along the front and back of this – make the lines considerably longer than the sides of the panel as they will be obscured by adhesive when you come to lay the panels. Repeat the process across the width of the room and you will now have the starting point for your central panel, central pair of panels or four central panels.

The individual panels are laid on a bitumen-based adhesive, starting in the centre of the room (as determined by the 'dry' setting out plan). Using a notched spreader, spread enough adhesive on the floor to lay the first panel (or the first two or four panels) and put in place; avoid getting any adhesive on the front face of the panel. Tap the panels in place lightly with a mallet, using an off-cut of timber to protect the surface. No adhesive

Woodstrip flooring can be used in many rooms in the home; used in a bedroom, it can provide a dramatic background to other furniture and furnishings.

is necessary with self-adhesive mosaic panels – simply peel off the backing paper and press the tile in place.

Work outwards from the centre until you are less than a full panel's width from the wall. Make sure the tongued-and-grooved joints are pushed together tightly. To cut the last panel to size, lay a whole panel on top of the last whole panel laid and then lay a second panel on top positioned so that it is 12.5 mm (½ in) away from the wall. Where the second panel meets the first panel is the cutting line, so draw down it with a pencil – see the diagram on page 45 and photographs on page 88. Now cut the first panel along the line and the cut-down panel should now fit exactly into the space available.

After fitting all the edging panels, fit cork expansion strips into the expansion gaps and replace the skirting board (baseboard) if you removed it; where skirtings were left in place, use quadrant or scotia moulding to cover the expansion gap, if you wish.

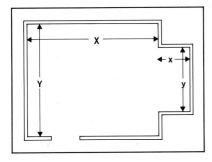

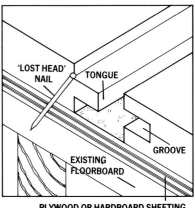

MEASURING UP

Measure the longest walls (X and Y) in metres or in feet (depending on how the flooring is sold). Calculate areas such as bays separately (here, add x times y) and add 5 per cent to the total answer. The length of expansion strip needed is 2X + 2Y + 2x.

LAYING WOODSTRIP FLOORING

A solid level base is essential for laying woodstrip flooring (especially the thinner types) and care should be taken to ensure this with floor levelling compound on a solid floor and hardboard or plywood sheeting on a suspended wooden floor. If a wooden floor has a slope on it (not uncommon in older houses), this, too, should have a floor levelling compound applied to it *after* the hardboard or plywood sheeting. Make sure you leave inspection hatches for access to pipes and wiring.

There are different types of woodstrip flooring and different ways of fitting them, so it is essential that you read the manufacturer's instructions before starting. Some thicker woodstrip floorings require a damp-proof membrane underneath them; other thinner types can be laid directly on a hardboard or plywood sheet.

Whichever method you are using, work out how many strips you will need to cover the room, allowing for a gap of 10 mm (3/8 in) at the wall or at the skirting (baseboard) if the skirting boards are being left in place. Woodstrip flooring is laid at right angles to the existing floorboards and parallel with the longest wall. Check how many strips will be needed to cross the room and, if the last strip will be less than 25 mm (1 in) wide, cut the first strip down as well, so that the first and last strip will be the same size.

Woodstrip flooring is tongued and grooved and the first row of strips (cut to a narrower width if necessary) is fitted 10 mm (3/8 in) away from one of the longer walls with its

CUTTING EDGE STRIPS

With mosaic flooring, lay a whole panel (B) exactly on top of the last whole panel (A) and then a further panel (C) with its edge 12.5 mm (1/2 in) away from the wall. Mark and cut out the shaded area from panel B so that it will fit into the space left.

groove (or cut edge) facing the wall and its tongue facing into the room. In order to position the first row correctly cut up a piece of 25 × 12 mm (1 × 1/2 in) timber (finished thickness 10 mm or 3/8 in) into 100 mm (4 in) lengths and slip these between the first row and the wall. You will need to cut one or more pieces of the flooring to length so that the row extends the full length of the wall – leave 10 mm (3/8 in) expansion gaps at the ends as well (see page 47 for some tips on cutting flooring).

Once the first row has been secured (see right and following page), the second one is put into place, making sure that the end joints between strips do not coincide with the joints in the first row and that the grooves of the second row strips are pushed over the tongues of the first row. You will need an off-cut of the flooring (with a groove on it) and a hammer to force the second strip tight up against the first one. When you get to the last row, the strips will have to be cut to the correct width (allowing for the expansion gap) and the strip manoeuvred into place fitting the groove over the previous row's tongue and finally forced into place with a lever or crowbar, using an off-cut of timber against the wall or skirting board (baseboard).

Fill the expansion gaps with cork strips and cover with quadrant or scotia moulding if wished (or re-fit the skirting boards). If necessary, apply a finish to the floor.

SECRET NAILING

When securing woodstrip flooring, punch the nail home at an angle so it will be covered by the next strip.

SECURING WOODSTRIP FLOORING

There are three methods of securing strip flooring: 'secret nailing', adhesive and clips.

SECRET NAILING This is a technique used when securing thick woodstrip flooring to an existing timber floor covered with hardboard or plywood sheeting or when using it to replace existing floorboards. When the first row of strips is laid, 'lost head' nails are hammered in at an angle through the tongue into the floor below (or, when replacing floorboards, into the joists) and the nails then punched home. Drilling pilot holes for the nails will prevent damaging the tongues. When the next row is fitted, the nails will be hidden. The last row of strips cannot be secret nailed: it will have to be nailed through the surface (like conventional floorboards) and the nail holes filled to match the flooring. With secret nailing, wood adhesive should be used on the tongued-and-grooved joints at the ends of strips in the same row. When nailing woodstrip flooring to joists to replace floorboards, make sure that each board is cut so that it finishes in the middle of a joist.

ADHESIVE You would use adhesive when laying woodstrip flooring on a solid floor. With this method, the woodstrip flooring is not actually secured to the sub-floor but is, in effect 'floating'. Normal PVA woodworking adhesive is used along the grooves in one row of strips before they are pushed over the tongues of the previous row – the usual application is a thin line of adhesive 100–200 mm (4–8 in) long every 500 mm (20 in) along the board. For the last row, put adhesive along the whole groove. Adhesive also needs to be applied to the end tongued-and-grooved joints.

CLIPS Some makes of woodstrip flooring have securing clips which fit into a special slot in the underside of each board to hold the boards together. The clip is hammered into place on the back of the first row of boards and will grip the second row when this is hammered gently into place. Adhesive should be used on the end joints, but not on the main joints, except for the *last* row of boards where adhesive should be used along the whole joint.

LAYING WOODSTRIP FLOORING WITH CLIPS

1 Once the sub-floor has been prepared, lay a special damp-proof membrane over the entire floor surface and tape it up the side walls.

2 Hammer the clips into the slot on the first row of boards in the direction of the tongue. Reduce the width of the board if necessary to avoid awkward cutting on the far side of the room.

3 Position the first row of boards in place, applying adhesive to the end joints and inserting 10 mm (3/8 in) spacing blocks between the boards and the walls. Place the second row, with its clips already attached, in position.

4 Gently hammer the edge of the second row, using an off-cut to protect the tongue, to push the clips on the first row on to those on the second row.

5 Continue in this way to complete the floor.

6 To finish off, remove the spacing strips and replace the skirtings (baseboards).

PROBLEMS WITH FITTING TIMBER FLOORING

No matter what type of timber flooring you are fitting, you are sure to encounter various difficulties along the way. The main problems will be cutting woodstrip flooring to size, fitting flooring around doorways and around pipes passing up through the floor and making access panels.

CUTTING WOODSTRIPS TO SIZE

When laying woodstrip flooring, you will have to cut quite a few boards to the correct length and at least one to the correct width.

Cutting to length is the most difficult as you must ensure that the cut is square and plan carefully so that you use all the pieces. If you start in one corner of a room, the first piece will have the groove on its long side and the groove on its end against the two walls. Assuming this piece will not reach the length of the room, you will have to cut down a second piece to fill the gap left. Mark the cutting line using a try square and keep your saw as straight and as square to the wood as possible. Make the mark so that the groove of the piece you are cutting will fit into the tongue of the piece already laid with the cut end against the wall. Now use the piece which is left as the first piece of the next row – that is, with its cut end against the first wall and its tongue ready to receive the next piece. This will minimize wastage.

When cutting a board down in width (to fill the last gap), the ideal tool for the job is a circular saw fitted with a guide which can be set to the exact width required. Then simply run the saw along the board, taking care at the end of the cut to keep on a straight line. Do a trial run first to make sure the guide is set correctly.

CUTTING AROUND PIPES

There is a special technique for fitting timber flooring around pipes. First measure exactly where the pipe will be on the board when it is in place and transfer this measurement to the board, drawing in the hole through which the pipe will pass. Hold the board against the pipe to double check that you have drawn the pipe in the right place. Now mark the centre of each hole and drill it out using a wood bit 3 mm (⅛ in) larger than the diameter of the pipe to allow for expansion.

When the hole has been drilled, make two angled cuts with a fine-toothed saw from the edge of the board to the sides of the hole so that a piece of the board can be removed. The board can now be put in place around the pipes and the piece you have cut out slotted in behind it, using glue on its two angled edges to secure it. Wipe off excess glue immediately with a damp cloth. With care, the fit should be perfect.

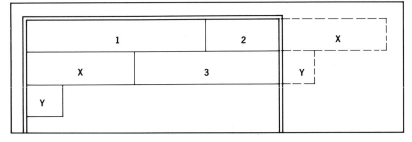

CUTTING BOARDS TO LENGTH

After laying length 1, cut length 2 so that it finishes 10 mm (⅜ in) short of the wall. The cut-off area (X) of piece 2 now becomes the first strip of the second row. In the same way, the cut-off area (Y) of piece 3 is used to start the third row.

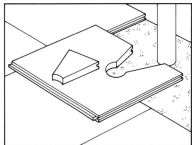

CUTTING AROUND A PIPE

After marking out and drilling a hole slightly larger than the pipe, make two angled cuts so that the cut-out piece can be glued in place behind the pipe once the main panel has been laid.

Left: Beech woodstrip flooring is an ideal floor covering for a kitchen.

FITTING AROUND DOORWAYS

Unless you are prepared to remove the door architraves at the same time as you remove the skirting, you will have difficulty cutting timber flooring to fit around them. However, you are likely to damage the architrave if you remove it, so be prepared to replace it if this is the route you intend to follow. The new architrave must be cut shorter by the thickness of the flooring, so that it sits on top. Alternatively, you may be able to cut through the architrave *in situ*, but this needs great care and a steady hand.

Finally, you could use a profile gauge to receive the shape of the architrave moulding and then transfer this to the flooring to cut out the shape with a jigsaw or coping saw. You will, of course, have to cut the flooring to fit in the doorway itself.

FINISHING OFF TIMBER FLOORING

Some timber floorings already have a protective vinyl layer on top and need no further finishing (although a single coat of varnish is usually recommended). With others, and with stripped and sanded conventional floorboards, you will want to apply a finish, not only to make the flooring look good, but also to keep it looking good, make it easy to clean and to protect it from general wear and tear.

With conventional floorboards and unsealed pine timber flooring, you can first use a wood stain to give the wood a deeper colour than its natural hue. There is a wide choice available from 'natural' wood colours, such as teak or mahogany, to the more exotic such as reds, yellows and greens.

You are unlikely to want to over-paint new timber flooring completely, but you might perhaps want to decorate it with stencilled patterns, using pastel shades. Wood stain stencilling could also be used for a more subtle effect.

The best-looking finish for a timber floor is undoubtedly a shellac and wax sealer, but this is hard work to apply, does not wear well and needs regular recoating with wax. An oleo-resin seal is tougher and will retain the character of the wood, but the most common type of finish is a polyurethane varnish. Hardwearing, resistant to heat and light, a polyurethane varnish or floor sealer is the most practical way to finish off a timber floor. Most manufacturers of timber flooring will recommend their own brand of floor sealer – or you could use a proprietary brand. Make

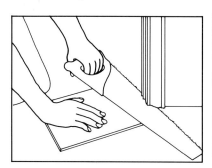

CUTTING THROUGH ARCHITRAVE

Use a piece of the flooring as a guide to cut through the door architrave so that the flooring can be fitted underneath.

Right: *A woodstrip floor treated with protective oil in the factory is easy to keep clean and will resist wear well. Additional treatment may be necessary in areas of particularly high wear.*

sure that you use a 'hard' polyurethane varnish which will withstand wear.

To prepare the surface for varnish, you may need to sand the wood surface (unless it is pre-sanded). Then follow the instructions on the varnish tin for its application – you will need at least three coats, allowing each coat to dry before applying the next one and, preferably, rubbing down with fine abrasive paper between each coat.

Expansion gaps left around timber flooring will generally be filled with cork expansion strip and covered by the skirting board (baseboard). But where they are visible, fit quadrant or scotia moulding to cover the strips. The moulding is pinned to the skirting (*not* to the floor) and can be painted to match the skirting or varnished to match the floor.

CUTTING INSPECTION HATCHES

Where you need access to underfloor pipes or electrical accessories, such as junction boxes, it is essential to leave inspection hatches in the floor. Pages 17 and 21 give details of how to do this for floorboards or sheet flooring; where a timber floor is added on top, cuts will be needed in this to line up with the inspection hatch.

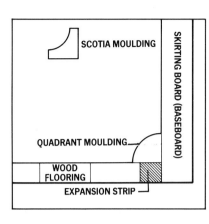

USING MOULDINGS

Where cork expansion strip is visible in front of a skirting board (baseboard), cover it with quadrant moulding or with scotia moulding (inset). Pin the moulding to the skirting board, not the floor.

Above: *Applying varnish to a stripped and sanded floor.*

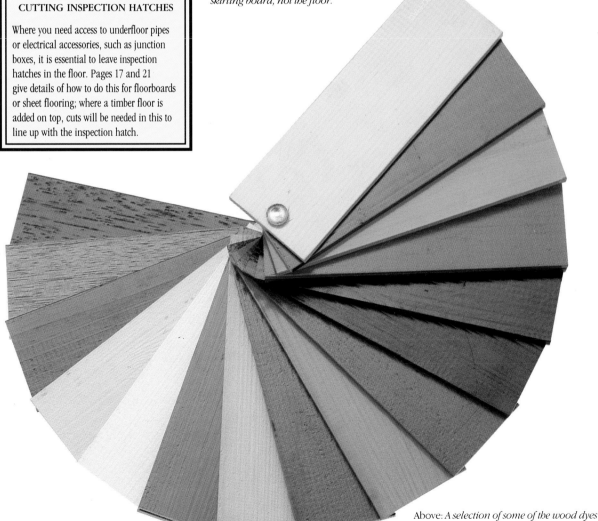

Above: *A selection of some of the wood dyes available.*

CARPETS AND SHEET FLOORING

 Carpet is a very popular way of covering floors. Luxurious and warm underfoot, it is quiet, can be colourful and adds considerably to the warmth of a room.

There are many different types of carpet on the market. They vary greatly in their construction, material and style, and your choice will depend on various factors.

The attractive border effect in these carpet tiles is achieved by laying adjacent tiles with their pile pointing in opposite directions and cutting into the tile diagonally at the corners of the border.

TYPES OF CARPETING

When choosing a new carpet there is one major factor you will be bearing in mind. Where is the carpet to be laid? If the site is a busy thoroughfare, such as a hallway, or a room which will see a lot of wear, such as a playroom, you will need a durable carpet. However, if it is for a bedroom, durability is not of prime consideration – you will probably choose the carpet purely on its looks and for underfoot comfort. If choosing carpeting for kitchens and bathrooms you will want both an easy-to-clean and water-resistant surface.

CARPET CONSTRUCTION

Carpets can be made in one of three ways: bonded, tufted or woven.

BONDED carpet, also known as 'needlefelt', has the fibres punched into an adhesive backing and heat is then applied to secure them. A second backing layer is then usually applied. Bonded carpets are fairly cheap to make and do not have any 'pile'. Carpet tiles are generally made this way.

TUFTED carpet, the most popular kind, has tufts of pile stitched into a pre-woven backing and then secured with latex adhesive. A second backing layer, sometimes incorporating a foam underlay, is then added to strengthen the carpet.

WOVEN carpet is the most expensive (and luxurious) type. Here the pile and the backing are woven together to produce a strong and durable result. Two different methods are used for the weaving process: *Axminster* carpets can cope with several different colours so can be richly patterned, while *Wilton* carpets generally have no more than five colours and are often made in a single colour from continuous strands of material.

CARPET MATERIALS

Carpets can be made from a wide variety of both natural and man-made materials. The most commonly used materials are wool, nylon, acrylic and polypropylene.

WOOL carpets are the most expensive, but resist wear well, are warm and soft and easy to clean. They are harder wearing when mixed with a synthetic fibre – 80 per cent wool and 20 per cent acrylic, for example.

NYLON carpets are extremely hardwearing and the more expensive types can feel nearly as soft as wool. Cheaper nylon carpets often attract dirt and feel harsh to the touch.

ACRYLIC carpets are cheaper than wool, but more expensive than nylon. They wear well and look and feel like wool. Acrylic fibres (often sold under brand names such as Acrilan, Courtelle, Dralon and Orlon) are often blended with other materials in carpet manufacture.

POLYPROPYLENE carpets are inexpensive and very durable, but can have a rather harsh feel. Polypropylene does not resist flattening well, so is often used in short pile carpets or in carpet tiles and may be incorporated with other fabrics.

MATTINGS

Mats made from natural fibres have been used for years as floor coverings and are now very popular in the home. The main fibres are **coir** (from coconut fibre), **sisal** (from tropical bushes) and **seagrass**. All come in a variety of colours, weaves and patterns and they are hardwearing, soft (though coir is a little 'hairy') and easy to clean.

The mattings are supplied with a latex backing (so no separate underlay is needed) and come in 4 m (13 ft) widths so they can be fitted from wall to wall. They are held down to the floor with adhesive, but do not need to be stretched.

RUGS

Carpet is generally designed to be fitted from wall to wall to cover a room completely. Rugs cover only part of the floor and can be an integral part of the room's interior design, especially if highly coloured and exotic rugs are used.

Almost every country has its traditional hand-made rugs – the cotton dhurry from India, for example, or Turkish, Persian and Turkoman rugs with their distinctive and colourful designs.

Modern machine-made rugs are less expensive, but can be very attractive and you may be able to get them made to order.

To preserve them, good-quality rugs should have an underlay fitted if they are going on bare wooden boards (though often, of course, they will be laid on the carpet). On hard floor surfaces, light rugs should be secured with mesh backing or nylon bonding strips to prevent them moving around and slipping when people tread on them.

CARPET UNDERLAYS
Use felt (1, 2) or rubber (3, 4) underlays for fabric-backed carpets and felt-paper underlay (5) for foam-backed ones. Felt and rubber underlays come in various grades and they should be matched to the type of the carpet you are laying, taking wear and insulation needs into account.

CHOICES

The range of carpets to choose from is wide; they are made from various natural and man-made materials and constructed in various ways. This aside, all types of carpets come in a glorious array of colours, patterns and textures. Sheet vinyl designs have become extremely sophisticated; many of them realistically simulate other types of floor coverings, such as tiles and woodstrip or woodblock flooring. Lino (linoleum) is once again becoming a popular floor covering, with new stylish colours and special border designs.

1 **Tufted 80/20 per cent wool/nylon carpets in plain colours**
2 **Sheet linoleum in various colours**
3 **Cushioned and solid sheet vinyl in various designs**
4 **Coir (coconut fibre) mattings, with varied colours and textures**
5 **Sisal mattings**
6 **Needlefelt acrylic carpets with textured design**
7 **Plain-coloured woven Wilton carpets**
8 **Patterned woven Axminster carpet**
9 **Wool carpet with integral border design**
10 **Foam-backed looped pile carpet**

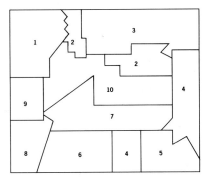

CARPET PILE

The pile of the carpet may be *looped* in and out of the backing or be *cut* – that is with the ends of the pile showing. Cut pile can have different lengths – long pile carpets are called 'shag pile', while very short pile varieties are known as 'velvet'. A tightly-looped pile is often called a 'corded' carpet. Axminster carpets are always cut pile, Wilton carpets can be either cut or looped pile. Note that shag pile carpets need regular attention and should never be used on stairs, where heels could catch in the pile.

CARPET LAYING EQUIPMENT
The photograph shows most of the tools and equipment you need for laying carpet.

1 Carpet tape For securing cuts made in carpet; often used in combination with *latex adhesive*.

2 Gripper strips Wooden strips with protruding angled spikes which are nailed into wooden floors or glued/nailed to solid floors.

3 Threshold strips For finishing carpet at doorways. Available in both single and double varieties and in a choice of finishes.

4 Knee-kicker The most important tool in laying carpet with a separate underlay. The flat sole at the front has adjustable teeth which are used to stretch the carpet when forcing it over gripper strips.

5 Tacks Used to secure carpet where it is not possible to use a gripper strip (especially on stair carpet).

6 Nails Used for holding down gripper strips on wooden floors (special nails used on solid floors).

7 Trimming knife Used for cutting carpet and underlay (a pair of heavy-duty scissors is also useful).

8 Tape measure Essential for measuring carpet to the right size.

9 Claw hammer Useful for removing tacks and can be used (with a nail punch) for putting down gripper strips.

10 Pin hammer A narrow-headed hammer which can be used for nailing down gripper strips without damaging the gripper pins (a carpet layer's hammer has a narrow heavy head).

11 Staple gun A quick and reliable way of securing underlay.

12 Seam roller Used for securing cut pieces of carpet on to tape and latex adhesive.

13 Double-sided adhesive tape Used for holding down foam-backed carpet. Available in two widths: 25 mm (1 in) for use at the edges of a room and 50 mm (2 in) for use where two pieces of carpet are to be joined.

14 Bolster (wide) chisel Used for pushing carpet down behind gripper strips and under the skirting board (baseboard).

15 Latex adhesive Can be applied to the cut edges of foam-backed carpet to prevent fraying. Also used to join two lengths of carpet in conjunction with carpet tape.

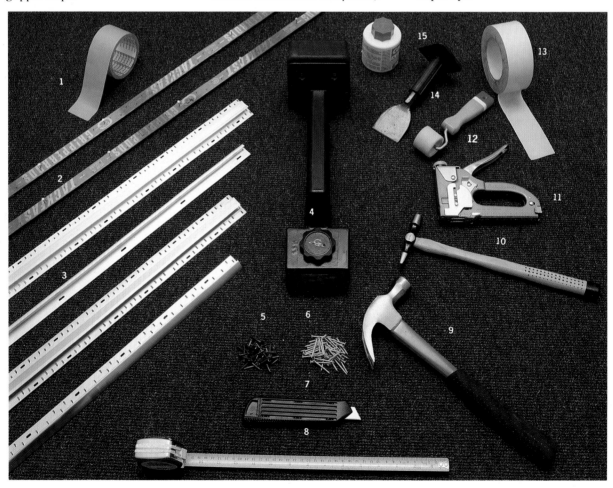

PREPARATION

The way you lay a carpet depends on whether or not it has a foam backing which acts as an underlay. Foam-backed carpet is laid straight on to the floor, usually with a paper underlay, and secured by double-sided adhesive tape with no stretching. Unbacked carpet needs a separate felt or rubber underlay to be put down first and the carpet then has to be stretched over it to be secured at the edges by tacks or by fitting it over gripper strips.

ESTIMATING CARPET

Carpet is sold by the square metre (or yard) and the standard roll width is 3.65 m (12 ft). So the first thing to do is to measure up the size of your room(s) to work out how much carpet you need.

Measure the width and length of each room at several points and draw a plan of the room (to a scale of 1:20) showing the position of doors and windows. Take this with you when you go to buy the carpet. A good carpet retailer will then be able to recommend the most economical layout to use, allowing a small amount (say 100 mm or 4 in) on the length and width to allow for fitting.

CUTTING CARPET TO SIZE

Before taking the carpet into the room, examine which way the pile runs. Ideally, it should be positioned so that the pile faces away from the main or only window and towards the door – this avoids shading. A carpet feels smooth when you run your hand along the carpet with the pile and provides resistance when you run your hand against the pile. If the carpet has a pattern, this should appear regular when looked at from the door as you come into the room.

If the carpet was not trimmed in the shop (or if it is a second-hand carpet), you should cut it roughly to size now – leaving a trimming allowance of around 25 mm (1 in) for foam-backed carpet and around 100 mm (4 in) for unbacked carpet (more if it has a pronounced pattern).

PREPARING THE SURFACE

Before laying carpet, the floor itself will need to be brought up to a good condition as described on pages 10–27.

A solid floor must be dry and relatively flat, though a carpet with a thick underlay can cope with slight irregularities; a timber floor must be sound with no rot, woodworm, loose or damaged boards, protruding nails or damp.

Unless it is very uneven, you will not need to level a solid floor, provided it is dry; an uneven timber floor could be covered with hardboard sheet nailed down to provide a base for carpeting. Skirting boards (baseboards) do not need to be removed, though it will usually be a good idea to take off doors, which may need to be shortened after the carpet has been laid.

You should take all the furniture out of the room before you start laying carpet and remove all old floor coverings. Take the opportunity to paint the skirting boards, a job which will be much easier with no floor covering to get in the way. If you are carpeting, you do not need to worry about getting splashes of paint on the floor.

A hardwearing polypropylene carpet can handle the traffic in a hallway and comes with a natural jute backing.

LAYING FOAM-BACKED CARPET

Carpet with its own built-in foam underlay is much easier to lay than carpet which has a separate underlay. No gripper strips need to be fitted, underlay does not have to be cut or fitted and no stretching of the carpet is involved.

If a timber floor is level enough not to need a hardboard covering before laying carpet, it should be covered with a paper underlay to prevent dirt blowing up between the floorboards and marking or damaging the carpet. Paper underlay will also stop the foam backing from sticking to the floorboards. Sheets of newspaper could be used, but proper paper underlay is inexpensive and is available from most carpet retailers.

Paper underlay comes in rolls and can be cut with scissors or a trimming knife. Starting at the end of the room, cut to size and lay out. Lay the next piece alongside, overlapping by around 25 mm (1 in). The last piece can be overlapped by more than this or cut down in width to size.

The paper underlay can be held down with double-sided adhesive tape (or with masking tape) or can be secured to the floor using a staple gun. It should be positioned just in from the skirting boards (baseboards) to allow room for the double-sided adhesive tape which secures the main carpet.

It is generally easier to lay foam-backed carpet as a single piece, though in larger rooms you will have to lay two or more pieces joined together.

LAYING A SINGLE FOAM-BACKED CARPET

Foam-backed carpet can shrink or stretch once it is laid out, so it is a good idea to cut it roughly to size, allowing around 25 mm (1 in) at each edge for cutting, and then to leave it for a few days before sticking it down to the floor. The carpet can be cut with a pair of scissors or with a trimming knife working from the back.

Where the carpet has to be fitted into an alcove or a bay, use the trimming knife to make a cut parallel with the sides of the alcove or bay, still allowing a 25 mm (1 in) trimming allowance.

Before securing the carpet, roll it up and position it in the room across the corners so that you can get at the floor in front of the skirtings (baseboards) to put down some

25 mm (1 in) double-sided adhesive tape. Normally, it is sufficient to have tape around the outside, but in large rooms, the carpet manufacturer may recommend having strips of tape across the room at intermediate points. Double-sided tape is easy to put down, but make sure you leave the top backing in place and press the tape firmly down on to the surface (a wallpaper seam roller will help here).

Now reposition the carpet in the correct place and roll it up to the wall. Push the carpet well into the join between the wall and the skirting, so that you can see where it needs to be cut and make the final cut with a sharp trimming knife – hold the knife at an angle away from the wall with the blade resting on the skirting to ensure an even cut. Apply latex adhesive to the cut edge to prevent the carpet from fraying.

Now roll the carpet slightly back and peel the top backing off the double-sided adhesive tape. Press the carpet down on to the tape making sure it reaches the wall and that it adheres firmly.

Where the carpet finishes at the doorway, screw down an aluminium cover strip to cover the carpet edge. On solid floors, drill holes for wallplugs to secure the screws.

If a radiator pipe passes up through the floor, you will have to fit the carpet around it. The best way to do this is with a piece of copper pipe the same size as the radiator pipe (usually 15 mm or ½ in), with one end sharpened. This can then be used with a rotary motion to cut a precise hole in the carpet (make sure this is in the right place) and a slot is then cut from the edge of the carpet to the hole to enable the carpet to be fitted around the pipe. Put down some extra pieces of double-sided tape around the pipe to hold the carpet in place.

A deep-pile tufted foam-backed carpet can be used in most rooms of the house and is easy to lay.

JOINING TWO CARPETS

Where there are two pieces of foam-backed carpet to lay, you will need a strip of 50 mm (2 in) double-sided adhesive tape at the point where they meet – any paper underlay should finish short of this length of tape rather than underneath it.

Butt the two pieces of carpet up against one another, checking that the edges meet all the way along. If not, overlap the two pieces by around 18 mm (¾ in) and then cut through *both* pieces with a sharp trimming knife, using a metal straight-edge as a guide and with a plank of wood under the carpet to prevent damage to the floor. The two narrow trimmed strips can then be removed leaving a perfect join.

Lay the larger of the two pieces of carpet first, centring it on the tape (with the top backing now removed). Apply latex adhesive all along the edge and then put the second piece of carpet in place along this join, removing any excess adhesive with a damp cloth or sponge. Then secure the edges of both pieces as described above.

LAYING FOAM-BACKED CARPET

◀ **1** The first step with fitting a foam-backed carpet is to cut it roughly to size, allowing around 25 mm (1 in) for final trimming.

▶ **2** When carpeting an alcove, make a cut parallel to the side of the alcove with a trimming knife, using a metal straight-edge and a wood plank to protect the carpet underneath.

◀ **3** Paper underlay will prevent dirt and dust blowing up into the carpet. Stick down double-sided adhesive tape all round the room.

▶ **4** Secure the carpet by pressing it down on to the double-sided adhesive tape. Use a trimming knife to fit the carpet neatly into the skirting (baseboard) or wall.

LAYING FABRIC-BACKED CARPET

Fabric-backed carpet with a separate underlay takes much longer to lay than foam-backed carpet.

There are two methods for securing this carpet – turn-and-tack and gripper strip. With the turn-and-tack method, the carpet overlaps the underlay by around 50 mm (2 in). The carpet is then turned back on itself and tacks are driven through the double thickness of carpet into the floor underneath. This method is not suitable for laying carpet on solid floors (unless masonry nails are used). It also has its disadvantages when used on wooden floors as each tack will produce an indentation in the carpet which not only collects dirt, but also looks unsightly.

The gripper method takes longer and costs more, but gives a much more satisfactory result. Here, wooden gripper strips are nailed all around the edge of the floor, with a gap of around 10 mm (⅜ in) between the gripper strip and the skirting board (baseboard) or wall. The carpet is then stretched on to the angled spikes in the gripper strip and the end tucked over into the gap. On solid floors, gripper strips can be glued into place.

Laying fabric-backed carpet can take a lot of skill to get the stretching absolutely right and with a new carpet you might think it not worth the effort – especially if the carpet retailer offers free fitting or fitting at low cost. However, if you are fitting second-hand carpet or carpet you have brought with you from a previous home (both of which will already have been stretched at least once), it is certainly worth attempting it yourself.

FITTING THE GRIPPER STRIPS

When your room has been measured up, the overall width and length (plus the dimensions of any alcoves) will tell you the total length of gripper strip needed (see the diagram on page 45). Gripper strip generally comes in 760 mm (3 ft) lengths, but can be cut easily with a tenon saw (backsaw) or tinsnips. Take care when handling gripper strips as the angled spikes are very sharp; use leather gloves when cutting gripper strips to length.

The gripper strips are put down with the angled spikes pointing towards the wall, with a gap of 10 mm (⅜ in) between the strip and the wall. Some gripper strips come pre-nailed; with others, you may have to add your own 25 mm (1 in) nails. Hammer the nails

down using a narrow pin hammer (or carpet layer's hammer) to avoid damaging the angled spikes – if you only have a large hammer, use a nail punch to drive the nails home. Cut the strips when you reach a corner and take small lengths of strip into alcoves, continuing along the back of the alcove with full-length strips. With curved bays, cut short lengths of strip, so you can roughly follow the shape of the bay. Where pipes pass through the floor, cut small lengths of strip to fit around the pipe and cut a hole in the carpet as described for foam-backed carpet.

At doorways, you will need to fit a threshold strip exactly at the carpet's edge. Single thresholds are used where carpet does not continue into the next room; double threshold strips are used where the same (or another) carpet goes on beyond the doorway.

Woven patterned carpets are available in a wide choice of colours and designs. The design shown here coordinates perfectly with the wallpaper and soft furnishings.

LAYING THE UNDERLAY

If you have not needed to put down hardboard to level a timber floor, it is worth putting down a paper underlay to prevent dirt and dust blowing up between the floorboards. (See *Laying a Foam-Backed Carpet*, pages 56–57, for details of how to do this.)

Felt or foam-rubber underlay comes in rolls and you should start laying it in one corner of the room, so that it fits into the corner between two gripper strips. On a timber floor, secure the underlay with a staple gun or with carpet tacks; on a solid floor, use double-sided adhesive tape. Cut the underlay to length so that it fits neatly at the other end of the room and cut smaller pieces to line alcoves. Adjacent pieces of underlay are butt-jointed together: it does not need to be stretched, but using a knee-kicker can make it easier to position the underlay correctly. The last piece of underlay will have to be cut down in width to fit the gap available.

LAYING THE CARPET

Unbacked carpet needs to be cut leaving a larger trim allowance than for foam-backed carpet – allow 100 mm (4 in) on each edge, more if the carpet has a pronounced pattern. It will be difficult to cut the carpet in the room in which it is to be laid, so do this in a larger room or, if it is fine, in the garden. Always remember the old do-it-yourself adage: measure twice, cut once.

Position the carpet roughly in the room where it is to be laid and if it has a pattern, line this up so that it looks right when viewed from the doorway. When you are happy with the position, trim it to length all the way round, so that it is about 10 mm (⅜ in) larger than the room size. Shape the carpet to fit alcoves as you go.

Start fixing the carpet in one corner of the room by pushing it on to the gripper strip. Now work up the longest wall, using the knee-kicker to tension the carpet and hooking the carpet on to the gripper strip at regular intervals. When you reach the corner, go about 300 mm (12 in) along the next wall and hook the carpet on to the gripper strip once again. Work back down the gripper strip on the long wall, pushing the carpet on to the strip with a thin piece of wood or a bolster (wide) chisel.

Now go back to the original corner and use the knee-kicker to stretch the carpet along the gripper strip on the shorter wall until you reach the corner, again going round the corner for 300 mm (12 in) and hooking on. Work back to the first corner, hooking the carpet on to the gripper strip.

Now you can start stretching in earnest. Commencing at the original corner, work across the room in strips towards the near wall, hooking on to the gripper strip when you reach the other side. Go back to the first corner again and this time work along the length of the room, stretching the carpet to the far gripper strip and hooking on (be prepared to adjust the fixings on the other side of the wall).

Finally go round the edges of the room making sure the carpet is firmly held by the gripper strip and the loose ends are pushed down between the gripper strip and under the skirting board (baseboard), using a bolster chisel to push it home. Cut excess carpet with a trimming knife for a snug fit.

Where threshold strip is used in a doorway, the carpet should be stretched into this in the same way, after which the top of the threshold strip is hammered down, using a piece of wood to prevent the metal strip being damaged.

JOINING CARPET

If you have had to cut the carpet at any point to aid fitting, use a non-adhesive carpet jointing tape to repair the joint after first smearing it with latex carpet adhesive. Use a wallpaper seam roller to press the two pieces of carpet down into the adhesive. Making large joins – between two pieces of carpet – requires skilled sewing and is not something you would tackle yourself.

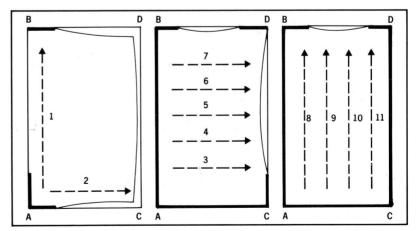

ORDER OF WORK

The arrows in this diagram denote the order of work when stretching fabric-backed carpet.

LAYING FABRIC-BACKED CARPET

1 Nail gripper strip down all around the edge of the room, leaving a 10 mm (⅜ in) gap behind it. If using a claw hammer, use a nail punch to drive the nails home.

2 Nail down a threshold strip across the doorways.

3 Tape or staple down paper underlay to stop dirt blowing up through the floorboards.

4 Cut the underfelt to fit inside the gripper strips and staple this to the floor.

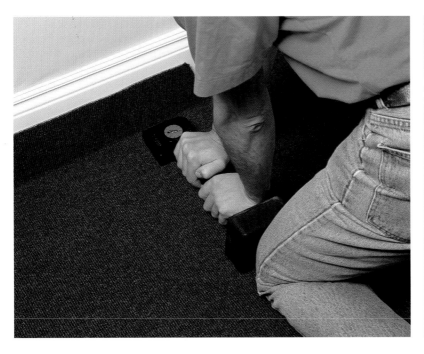

5 Leaving a generous allowance for trimming, use the knee-kicker to stretch the carpet up to the gripper strips.

6 Cut through the carpet at the skirting board (baseboard) with a sharp trimming knife.

7 Push the trimmed carpet down behind the gripper strip and under the skirting board, using a clean bolster (wide) chisel.

8 Where carpet has been cut to aid fitting, repair the joints using adhesive and a seaming tape.

9 The completed result – neat wall-to-wall 'fitted' carpet.

CARPETING STAIRS AND STEPS

Laying carpet on stairs is not much more complicated than laying it on flat surfaces, but you do need to follow a few basic rules. Before commencing, check whether your stairs need any of the repairs described on pages 22–23. Some of these, such as stopping stairs creaking, can be carried out after the carpet has been laid, provided there is access to the underside of the stairs; others, especially repairing worn nosings, must be carried out before the carpet is laid.

MEASURING UP

You will probably have to cut the carpet for your stairs from a larger piece, so it is essential to measure the stairs carefully. You will need separate pieces of carpet for:
- the hall at the bottom of the stairs
- the landing at the top of the stairs
- runs of straight stairs
- any part landings if the stairs curve
- winder stairs (where the stairs go round a corner)
- bullnoses (a shaped stair at the bottom of the flight).

The amount needed for straight flights is the sum of the treads (the horizontal parts of the stairs) and the risers (the vertical segments), excluding the top riser. The top riser should be covered by the landing carpet. Allow 32 mm (1¼ in) extra on the width for the landing and stair carpet to turn over where it meets the banisters.

For winder stairs, you need a rectangle of carpet equal to the two largest dimensions of the winder – the riser plus the tread measured across the corners with the width also measured across the corners, allowing 32 mm (1¼ in) for turning over.

With a bullnose stair, you need to add more to the width to allow for turning the carpet round the corner.

The direction of the pile on a stair carpet should be *down* the stairs.

FITTING GRIPPER STRIPS

On stairs, you need to fit gripper strips to the back of each tread (except the top step below a landing) and to the bottom of each riser so that they form a pair of 'jaws' to hold the carpet in place. These start at the wall, but finish around 32 mm (1¼ in) short of the banisters to allow room for turning the carpet over. Gripper strip is also fitted to the wall side on winder stairs, but not on straight stairs. Hallways and landings need gripper strip fitted all along the walls as described on page 58, except for the edge of a landing next to the banisters, where the carpet is turned over and tacked.

LAYING THE UNDERLAY

Start fitting underlay on the landings and in the hall as described before, but on a landing finish 32 mm (1¼ in) short of the banisters. Allow a short piece of underlay from the landing to overlap the riser of the top stair and staple this just below the nosing. Trim the underlay, cutting it off short of the gripper strip on the riser.

For straight stairs, cut a length of underlay to the width of the stairs less 32 mm (1¼ in) for the rolled edge. Lay the whole length down the stairs, with one edge against the wall, and start fitting it from the top stair. Staple underlay so that it fits snugly next to the gripper strip on the top stair tread and then staple it again just below the nosing on the riser below. Use a trimming knife to cut across the width of underlay – you do not need to fit it all down the riser. Then go to the next stair and so on to the bottom.

You can use the same carpet on the stairs as on the main floor. Here, a 80/20 per cent wool/nylon carpet (used with a matching border on the main floor) maximizes comfort and wear.

LAYING THE STAIR CARPET

The hall carpet and landing carpet should be laid first in the way described on pages 58–61. Where the landing meets the stair banisters, turn over the edge of the carpet, so that the fold fits neatly against the banisters, and nail carpet tacks through both thicknesses. Take the flap allowed for the first riser over the top nosing and push the end over the gripper strip at the bottom of the top riser, forcing the carpet into the corner. Trim any carpet off the end first if necessary and fold over the edge running along the banisters and hammer tacks into the riser to secure it. It will help to make the fold if you cut the bottom corner off at an angle.

Now lay your carpet strip down the stairs and fold over the edge next to the banisters. Start laying the stair carpet by folding over the top edge and pushing it under the flap from the landing you have already secured to the top riser. Use carpet tacks to secure this all along its back edge. Making sure the carpet is a snug fit on the wall side (where it is not secured), check the fold at the banister side to make sure it is right up against the banisters and nail this folded edge in place with carpet tacks. Put in more tacks down the banister side of the next riser down and then push the strip into the corner between this riser and the next tread. Force this into place, using a clean bolster (wide) chisel and a rubber mallet. Work down the stairs like this, checking that the carpet is straight, until you get to the bottom. On a straight bottom step, the carpet is secured to the gripper strip fitted at the bottom of the riser and, for security, tacked into place as well (the hall carpet fits *below* the gripper strip).

With a bullnose stair, you will need to cut the carpet carefully to fit it round the newel post and to take it round the curve of the bullnose. Tack it into place all round the bullnose on the riser.

laid first in the way described on pages 58–61.

WINDER STAIRS

When laying fitted carpet to winder stairs, it is best to cut a separate piece for each winder. Line the piece up with the bottom of the riser and force it over the gripper strip here before folding it over the nosing and cutting it with a trimming knife run along the corner where it meets the wall. Then secure it to the gripper strip on the wall side of the winder tread. To make folding the carpet easier at the inside corner, cut a small 'V' from the edge. Finally, cut the top edge to shape and force it over the gripper strip at the back of the tread, trimming it to the final shape if necessary.

LAYING STAIR CARPET

1 For stair carpet, fit gripper strips along the back of the tread and base of the riser to form a pair of 'jaws'.

2 Staple the underlay in place, cutting it short of the gripper strip on the riser and leaving a gap at the banister edge.

3 Start laying carpet at the top of the stairs, working your way down one stair at a time.

4 Use a rubber mallet and a clean bolster (wide) chisel to force the carpet into the corner between tread and riser.

LAYING CARPET TILES

The big plus for carpet tiles is that if one tile gets damaged, it can easily be replaced. Also, most carpet tiles are washable, so are ideal for use in a kitchen, bathroom or child's room. As an added bonus they are easy to lay.

Usually carpet tiles are squares of bonded needlefelt carpet, but you can get carpet tiles made from a variety of materials, including coir (coconut matting).

ESTIMATING

As with any other type of flooring, the first task is to measure up the room to work out how many tiles you need. Carpet tiles come in standard sizes – typically 400 mm (16 in) or 500 mm (20 in) square – so it is easy to work out how many you will need.

Depending on the shape, size and layout of your room, decide whether you would prefer to start with whole tiles along the most visible walls (with a cut-down edge tile on the opposite side) or to centre the tiles (see *Marking the Start Position*, above right) with equal borders on both sides. Ideally, equal borders should not be less than a half tile in width, although if you do have thin borders you may be able to use all or part of the cut tiles elsewhere in the room.

Allow 5 per cent or so extra for mistakes made in cutting and for future replacement, remembering that carpet tiles are usually sold in packs rather than individually.

PREPARING THE SURFACE

Carpet tiles can be laid on both solid and suspended timber floors, but because they are relatively thin, are better suited to a level surface. This means correcting any bias with floor levelling compound on a solid floor and at least a covering of hardboard on a timber floor. Deal with all faults in the sub-floor first as described on pages 10–27.

LAYING THE TILES

Assuming you have calculated the number of tiles needed and decided on equal borders, 'snap' chalk lines along the centre of the room in both directions. To do this, cover a string line with French chalk, fix it tightly at the centre of two facing walls at floor level and then pick it up and let it drop. You now have the starting point for the carpet tiles.

A selection of carpet tiles, including, on the left, tiles made from a blend of coir and sisal.

Carpet tiles are laid 'dry' – that is, with no adhesive or tape. However, the *first* tile (in the centre of the room) should be laid on adhesive (or double-sided adhesive tape), so that it stays still during the subsequent laying process. If you are worried about other tiles moving, you could fit double-sided adhesive tape to, say, every third row across the middle of each tile.

Working out from the centre tile, carpet tiles are normally laid so that adjacent tiles have the pile running in opposite directions – an arrow on the back of the tile indicates the direction of the pile. If there is no arrow, you can feel for the pile direction. To give the appearance of fitted carpet, tiles should be laid with their pile in the same direction. Many people lay carpet tiles of more than one colour for a more decorative effect.

You should be able to push each tile up to fit flush against its neighbours, but you could use a knee-kicker (see page 59) to ensure a really snug fit.

When all the whole tiles have been laid, cut some tiles to fit the gaps left at the edges, using the technique shown in the photographs on page 88. To cut a carpet tile, make two nicks on the edges with a trimming knife. Then turn the tile over and line up the nicks with a metal straight-edge and use this as a guide for your trimming knife.

Where tiles have to be cut to fit around a pedestal basin or a WC in the bathroom, make a card template which fits exactly around the basin or WC and then transfer the shape to the tile and cut around it. You may

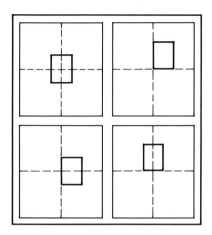

MARKING THE START POSITION
With chalk lines marking the centre of the room, there is a choice of four positions to put your first tile.

find, however, that pedestal basins and WCs can be loosened sufficiently from the floor to tuck the carpet tile underneath, which will give a much better effect. Cut carpet tiles as described on page 87 to accommodate pipes passing up through the floor.

At a doorway, use a profile gauge to transfer the shape of the door architrave on to the tile (remember to turn the gauge over as you are cutting the tile from the back) and cut through the tile with scissors (see page 87). Fit a metal threshold strip to protect the edges and prevent the tiles from moving.

SHEET FLOORING

The most popular type of sheet flooring is vinyl (also available as tiles – see page 70). This is available in both solid and 'cushioned' versions – cushioned vinyl is more comfortable and easier to maintain, though solid types are likely to last longer.

Vinyl flooring is a very practical surface as it resists stains and spillages well, is easy to brush or wipe clean and cushioned versions, in particular, effectively deaden noise. This makes it ideal for use in kitchens, bathrooms and children's bedrooms, but modern designs make it possible to use it in any room. Some vinyls may, however, not be able to cope with a lot of 'traffic' and will wear quickly.

Lino (linoleum), once very popular, is having something of a revival, and is now available in a wide range of styles and colours. It is warm to the touch and hardwearing, so is ideal in hallways and other areas of high traffic. If polished, it is easy to clean, so it is also suitable for kitchens. Lino, too, comes in tiles as well as sheets – see page 69. However, sheet lino is difficult for the amateur to lay as it is heavier, less flexible and harder to cut than vinyl.

Above: *Modern sheet lino can be laid with some stunning border effects.*

Below: *Cushioned vinyl provides warmth and comfort in a bathroom.*

PREPARING THE SURFACE

Sheet flooring needs to be laid on a dry flat floor, which should be prepared in the same way as for laying carpet (see page 55) with any remedial work being carried out as described on pages 10–27.

On uneven timber floors, lay down hardboard sheeting; on uneven solid floors, use floor levelling compound.

ESTIMATING QUANTITIES

Vinyl sheet comes in standard width sheets – typically 2 m (6 ft 6 in), 3 m (9 ft 8 in) and 4 m (13 ft) wide – so it should be possible to order a single piece to fit most bedrooms, bathrooms and kitchens without having a seam. This will certainly look better than having a join, but it does make the sheet a little cumbersome to lay. Lino is generally 2 m (6 ft 6 in) wide.

You will need to measure the room carefully, making sure that the sheet you buy is the longest length and the longest width necessary. Draw a 1:20 scale plan of your room and before taking the sheet into the room, lay it out in a larger room and draw the measurements on it allowing 100 mm (4 in) for trimming along all edges. Cut the sheet to size using scissors or a sharp trimming knife and straight-edge. Roll the sheet up to give the shortest length of roll and leave it in the room where it is to be laid for a couple of days to acclimatize.

TOOLS AND EQUIPMENT

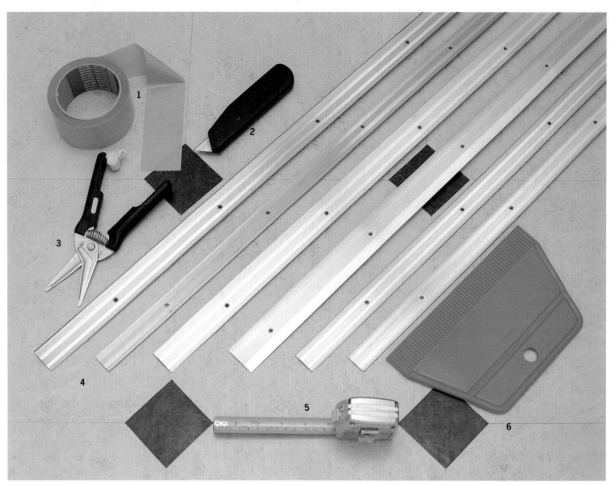

1 **Adhesive tape** For making joins and repairing cuts.

2 **Trimming knife** For trimming sheet at the edges.

3 **Multi-purpose scissors** For cutting sheets to size (more efficient than normal scissors).

4 **Threshold strips** For screwing down over the sheet where it finishes in a doorway.

5 **Tape measure** Essential for measuring the room accurately.

6 **Spreader** Used for applying adhesive to the floor surface where necessary.

LAYING SHEET VINYL

It is not easy to unroll a single piece of sheet vinyl big enough to cover the whole room on your own, so get someone to help you at this stage. Make sure the sheet is positioned the correct way round and, where there is a pattern, use the doorway as a view point to check that this looks straight.

To help the vinyl sheet lay flat, make cuts at the corners and then use a broom all over the surface. Next cut the vinyl so that there is an overlap of around 50 mm (2 in) at each wall for final trimming. In alcoves, make cuts parallel to the sides of the alcove and do the same for doorways.

Before the final trimming, cut the vinyl once more so that there is only around 25 mm (1 in) left to trim and use a square block of timber to force the vinyl sheet into the corner between the floor and the skirting board (baseboard). Now, using a steady hand, run the trimming knife all along the join between

the wall and skirting, holding the blade at an angle to the wall. Alternatively, fold the sheet back so you can mark the joining point and then cut along your marks with scissors.

Cut the sheet carefully to fit around the door architrave and into the doorway, finishing off underneath the door.

With 'stay-flat' vinyl sheets, you do not need to stick them down in any way; other types of vinyl sheet need to be glued down using a solvent-based adhesive. Cushioned vinyls need sticking down only at the edges, which simply means rolling them back, applying the adhesive and then sticking the edges down again. Solid types need gluing all over which you should do half a room at a time. Use a soft broom to press the vinyl down flat again.

Fit a threshold strip across the doorway, screwing it down to the floor underneath – on solid floors, fit wallplugs into the floor to take the screws.

SCRIBING

Where you want to lay sheet flooring to fit exactly against an irregular wall surface, you can use a procedure known as 'scribing'. For this you will want a short block of wood and a pencil. The sheet is then positioned away from the wall (by at least the size of the wood block) and the block is slid along the wall, with the pencil held against its far edge. This will reproduce the shape of the wall faithfully on the sheet so that you can get an exact fit.

MAKING JOINS

If you do need to join two sheets of vinyl flooring, first overlap them by at least 25 mm (1 in), but so that any pattern matches up exactly. Then, using a trimming knife and a straight-edge, cut through both layers at the same time. This will guarantee a perfect join. Where the vinyl is not glued to the floor, use double-sided adhesive tape to reinforce the join.

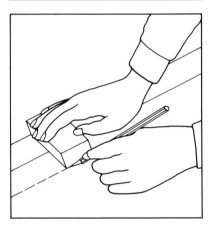

SCRIBING

Use a block of wood and a pencil to 'scribe' the edge of a flooring sheet to fit an irregular wall surface.

LAYING SHEET VINYL

1 Lay the sheet vinyl roughly in place and make cuts at the corners to enable it to lay flat.

2 With the pattern correctly positioned (as viewed from the door), make a mark on the sheet 25 mm (1 in) from the edge.

3 Cut the sheet down, using your marks, with a pair of scissors.

4 Now fold back the vinyl, holding it flat against the floor, and mark where it meets the skirting (baseboard). Trim finally with scissors along this line or with a trimming knife after pushing the vinyl into the corner between floor and skirting with a square block of wood.

5 Apply adhesive if necessary and go over the whole surface with a soft broom.

6 When laid, the vinyl sheet should be neatly tucked under the skirting board or, if there is no gap, flush against it.

TILES

You may think tiles are just the small, hard, glazed objects you put on kitchen and bathroom walls, but there is an enormous variety of tiles available, in a range of materials suitable to cover walls, floors or ceilings in any room in the house.

One advantage of tiles over sheet materials is that they are easier to handle, especially if they need to be fitted into an awkward space.

Traditional ceramic wall tiles are perfect when teamed with clay pottery and earthenware jugs. Random hand-painted feature tiles and narrow border tiles all add authenticity.

TYPES OF TILE

Tiles offer a wide variety of colour, texture, pattern and style and, by having the material in small pieces, it is easy to mix and match different colours and designs for some truly individual effects. Here is a résumé of the many diverse tiles available to the home decorator.

BRICK/STONE Many people like a natural brick effect on their walls and this can be achieved with thin brick or stone 'tiles' which are stuck on to the surface. Some of these are in fact thin sections cut from real bricks; others are moulded, which can look quite authentic for brick, but a little unconvincing for stone (the material is reconstituted stone). These tiles are not suitable for floors – here you should use the real thing.

CARPET The advantage of carpet tiles over sheet carpet is that you can replace an individual tile when it is badly stained or worn. Carpet tiles are covered in more detail on page 64.

CERAMIC The most familiar tile, available in different versions for walls and floors – the floor types are thicker and stronger. Ceramic tiles are extremely hardwearing and easy to clean, which makes them ideal for kitchens and bathrooms. Most tiles have a glazed surface, though some unglazed versions are sold for use on floors as they are non-slip. A ceramic tile surface is cold which, combined with their hardness, can make them tiring to stand on for long periods.

Most ceramic tiles in a do-it-yourself store will be machine made in standard sizes, but specialist tile shops offer a variety of hand-made designs in a range of sizes, shapes and individual patterns.

Putting ceramic tiles up on the wall or down on the floor takes time and a little practice; the most difficult part is cutting tiles to fit borders and around objects without cracking them. Although extremely tough, ceramic tiles are also very brittle.

The most common type of wall tile is square – typically 104 mm (4¼ in) or 150 mm (6 in) – though you can get oblong, hexagonal, octagonal, diamond and interlocking curved shapes. Floor tiles are usually larger – typically 200 mm (8 in) square.

Special heat-resistant types are available for worktops, and for floors subject to low temperatures there are frost-resistant types.

Ceramic tiles are held in place with adhesive (special water-resistant adhesives are also available) and the gaps between them need to be 'grouted' – filled with a special plaster. Different adhesives (and grouts) are used for wall and floor tiles.

CORK This is a very popular way of finishing both floors and walls. As with ceramic tiles, cork floor tiles are thicker and stronger than those used on walls, but the technique for laying them is the same.

Cork provides a warm surface, helps deaden noise and provides an attractive finish. Some cork tiles come ready-sealed with a PVC or acrylic coating; others need coating with polyurethane varnish.

Cork tiles are generally 300 mm (12 in) square and easy to fit and very easy to cut with a sharp knife. They are held in place with adhesive; some makes are self-adhesive.

LINO Linoleum is again becoming popular as a flooring material – this time as tiles (though sheet lino, quite different from the traditional material, is also available – see page 65). Lino is made from natural ingredients – including linseed oil, cork and wood – which are baked and compressed on to a backing material. It is difficult to lay in sheets, but lino tiles have been specially made so that they are stable. The usual size is 300 mm (12 in) square, but other shapes (mainly octagonal with small contrasting infill or inset squares) are also available.

Lino comes in an excellent range of rich colours and patterns and many exciting border tiles for floors are available. It is hardwearing and warm underfoot.

Lino tiles are stuck down to the floor surface with special adhesive – different from that used for *vinyl* floor tiles – and some are self-adhesive.

MINERAL FIBRE For use on ceilings, these tiles provide both heat and sound insulation. Available in both plain and textured versions, they can either be glued to the ceiling or, if tongued and grooved, secretly stapled through the tongues.

MIRROR As an alternative to sheet mirrors, mirror tiles come with a silver, bronze or 'smoke' finish. Like mirrors, they can be used to make rooms look larger or smaller or to reflect light. They will not give a perfect reflection unless laid on an absolutely flat surface. The normal size is 300 mm (12 in) square and the tiles are fixed to the surface with self-adhesive pads.

MOSAIC These are smaller versions of ceramic tiles and usually come joined together on a paper or mesh backing. They have the advantage over ceramic tiles that they can be fitted to curved surfaces and into irregular-shaped areas with ease. The panels of tiles (with grouting gaps already built in) are larger than single ceramic tiles, so are quicker to put up.

POLYSTYRENE Expanded polystyrene tiles are used mainly on ceilings. They help reduce heat loss and prevent condensation on an otherwise cold surface and are available in both plain and embossed styles. For safety, fire-resistant types should be used (especially in kitchens) and polystyrene tiles should never be painted over with a solvent-based gloss or eggshell paint. Polystyrene tiles are easy to cut with a sharp knife and are fixed to the ceiling with adhesive (all over the back, not just at the corners).

QUARRY AND TERRACOTTA A traditional flooring material, quarry tiles are extremely hardwearing and come in a range of warm, earthy colours – mainly reds and buffs. They are less likely to crack than ceramic tiles and have a matt non-slip surface. Quarry tiles are available in square, rectangular and hexagonal shapes; they can have a smooth or a textured surface. Both machine-made and hand-made tiles are available; hand-made quarries, which vary in thickness, are much more difficult to lay. Machine-made tiles are laid on a cement-based adhesive and can be used outside as well as inside.

Terracotta tiles are similar, but are warmer and quieter underfoot. As they are porous, they need sealing.

RUBBER Originally used for office and shop flooring, rubber tiles are becoming more popular for use in the home. They are hardwearing, but provide a quiet and soft surface to walk on; the surface has a texture (or 'studs') to make it non-slip. Only a limited range of plain colours is available but one advantage of rubber tiles is that they are fairly easy to lay. The 500 mm (20 in) square tiles are held down with a special two-part epoxy adhesive.

STONE For a really traditional look, there is nothing to beat a stone 'flag' floor. Stone floor tiles can be made from natural stone, marble and slate but, unlike quarry tiles, they are porous and must be sealed with a resin sealer to prevent them staining.

Stone tiles are extremely durable, but cold underfoot, noisy and heavy. In addition, they are difficult to lay.

VINYL One of today's most popular flooring materials, plain and cushioned vinyl is available in tile form as well as sheet (see page 65). They have the advantage of being cheap and easy to lay and are warm, comfortable, quiet and provide good insulation. The widely available type of vinyl tile has a printed pattern between a vinyl backing and a tough clear vinyl surface. More resilient types, designed for professional laying, are solid and less flexible, but come in designs which can look very much like traditional materials, such as brick, cork, slate or quarry tiles. The normal size is 300 mm (12 in) square, but shapes (mainly octagonal with small contrasting infill squares) are also available. Vinyl tiles are held down with adhesive; some types are self-adhesive.

CHOICES

Wall and floor tiles are available in an astonishing range of materials, sizes, shapes and designs. A sample selection is shown here, with the more unusual ones identified and listed below. Those not listed include both machine, hand-made and hand-painted tiles.

1 **Large ceramic floor tiles**
2 **Limestone floor tile**
3 **Hand-made terracotta floor tile**
4 **Cork floor tile**
5 **Chinese slate floor tile**
6 **Mirror tile**
7 **Marble floor tile**
8 **Glazed inset floor tile**
9 **Hexagonal terracotta floor tile**
10 **Slate inset floor tile**
11 **Shaped wall tile**
12 **Inset wall tile**
13 **Wall tile with matching border**
14 **Coordinating plain and patterned wall tiles with dado (chair) rail tile**
15 **Quarry tile**

PREPARING FOR TILING

How you approach a tiling job depends very much on the type of tiles to be used and the surface they are to be laid on. Putting ceramic tiles up on a wall, for instance, is quite different from laying vinyl tiles on a floor, while laying quarry tiles on a floor is equally different from putting cork tiling on a wall. The specific instructions and advice on the different materials is given in the relevant sections on *Tiling Walls* and *Tiling Floors*, but there are some general points which are covered here.

TOOLS AND EQUIPMENT

The photograph shows some of the tools you need for tiling – most of these are for ceramic tiling, the most popular job.

Tile cutters Many tiles (such as vinyl, lino and cork) can be cut with a sharp trimming knife. For the harder tiles, however, a special tile cutter is needed. Ceramic wall tiles can be cut by scoring the surface and then using a **tile snapper** (1), which breaks the tile along the scored line. These come in different versions – heavy-duty metal snappers and light-duty plastic varieties. For ceramic floor tiles and quarry tiles, you will need to hire or buy a **tile cutting machine** (2), which will avoid breaking tiles. For cutting mirror tiles, you will need a glass cutter.

3 **Tile saw** For cutting awkward shapes out of ceramic tiles, a tile saw has a thin circular abrasive blade. It is slow work and any attempt to force the cut will break the blade, but this is the best tool for cutting out notches for the ends of windowsills and L-shapes to fit around electric sockets.

4 **Abrasive paper** For smoothing the cut edges of ceramic tiles, silicon carbide abrasive paper can be used. Alternatives are a tile file, and a carborundum block.

5 **Pliers** These can be used to 'nibble' away pieces of ceramic tile when, for example, a cut is made close to the edge and the tile cannot be snapped. Pincers could also be used for this.

6 **Edging strip** A neat way of finishing off the edge of ceramic tiling – see page 79 for details of how it is fitted.

7 **Adhesive spreader** Often supplied with the adhesive for floor and wall tiles, the spreader has notches in it to leave ridges of adhesive on the wall or floor. This example has a squeegee blade on the far side.

8 **Squeegee** Used for applying grout to ceramic tiled surfaces. The flexible rubber blade will push the grout into the gaps between tiles and wipe excess grout off the surface. The heavy-duty squeegee shown here would be hard work to use on ceramic wall tiling, but is ideal for use with quarry tiles.

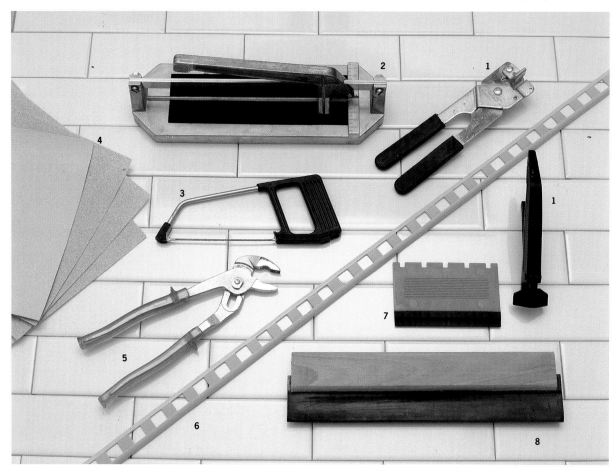

ADDITIONAL TOOLS

Other useful tools include: a **spirit level** for setting out tiles on a wall and checking the slope on floors; a **chalk line** to mark the centre lines on floors; a **plumb line** to establish true verticals on walls; **battens** (furring strips) to help with the putting up of wall tiles; a **gauge stick** for setting out tiles; a **scribing tool** and a **profile gauge** for reproducing shapes; a **steel float** for spreading cement-based adhesives on a floor; a metal **straight-edge** for guiding tile cutters and trimming knives when cutting tiles; **filling knife** for making repairs to walls before tiling and a **steel tape measure** for measuring up – do not use a cloth tape measure.

These stoneware floor tiles have a lovely antique hand-washed glaze and are perfect for use in a conservatory.

ESTIMATING AND SETTING OUT

In order to work out how many tiles you need to cover a particular floor or section of wall, you need to know the *area* (in square metres or feet) that you want to cover. This can be calculated simply by multiplying the width by the length. For floors with alcoves, add in the areas of the alcove separately; for bathrooms with vanity units, subtract the floor area taken up by the unit.

Then, if you know the size of each tile, you can work out its area allowing for one grouting gap of 2 mm (³⁄₃₂ in) on each dimension of a ceramic tile and 6 mm (¼ in) on each dimension of a quarry floor tile. Divide the area to be tiled by the area of one tile to give you the amount needed. To this you should add 5 per cent to allow for breakages and wastage.

Some packs of tiles helpfully give details of the area that a whole pack will cover; tubs of adhesive and grout will also give the area that they will cover.

Always work out how the tiles will fall, so you can see whether to have one slightly smaller tile at one edge or two considerably smaller tiles at both edges – you will not normally want to have edge tiles less than a half of a tile's width.

Floor tiles can be laid out 'dry' – that is, without any adhesive – to check the layout,

but for wall tiles it is a good idea to use a 'gauging stick'. This is simply a length of wood, with a series of marks representing the spacing of tiles (allowing for grouting where required). By holding this against the wall, you can see exactly how many tiles you will need for the length and the width and where the short tiles will fall. As a piece of wood has four edges (two on each side), you could mark out four different tile widths on it – say 108 mm (4¼ in), 150 mm (6 in), 200 mm (8 in) and 300 mm (12 in). The diagram below shows how a gauging stick can be used.

PREPARING THE SURFACES

All surfaces which are to be tiled need to be sound, dry and flat (and, in the case of floors, level). How flat they need to be depends on the type of tile to be laid. Quarry tiles, for instance, are laid on a fairly thick bed of cement-based adhesive which can cope with minor irregularities in a solid floor surface. On the other hand, thin cork tiles need a very flat surface as they will show any irregularities. The flattest surface of all is needed for mirror tiles where the reflection will show the slightest bump.

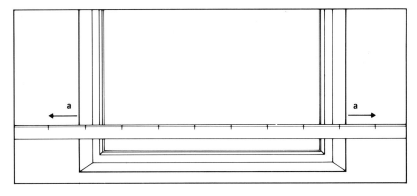

SETTING OUT
Use a gauging stick to even up tiles either side of a window. The two distances 'a' should be equal.

TILING WALLS

Tiling can be seen as another way of decorating a wall – that is, as an alternative to using paint or wallcoverings.

Ideal for kitchens and bathrooms, ceramic tiles give a practical, hardwearing and easy-to-clean surface; alternatively, cork tiles give a warmer and more mellow surface. In living rooms and bedrooms, you might want to use mirror tiles for reflecting light or changing the apparent shape of the room, cork for warmth or ceramics for effect.

Whatever your reason for tiling, the first essential is to ensure that the wall surface is sound.

PREPARING WALLS

Look to see how the wall you want to tile has been previously decorated. This will determine what you do next.

WALLPAPERED WALLS You cannot tile over a wall which has been covered with wallpaper or other types of wallcovering, such as vinyl. So any wallcovering will have to be removed first.

Some vinyl wallcoverings are designed to be peelable – that is, they peel away leaving just a backing paper attached to the wall. To remove this and ordinary wallpaper, first soak the paper with water using a sponge or large paint brush (to soften the adhesive) and then strip it off using a flat-bladed scraper. A proprietary wallpaper stripping chemical (or washing-up liquid/dishwashing detergent)

will help the water penetrate the paper. With painted wallpaper or vinyl-coated (washable) wallpaper, you will need to score the surface first, with a serrated scraper or wire brush, so that the water can get through.

If you are tiling only a section of the wall and do not want to repaper the rest, use a sharp trimming knife and a straight-edge to cut through the existing wallcovering around the area to be tiled and then only remove the wallcovering from within that area.

PAINTED WALLS You can tile directly on to walls which have been painted with an emulsion (latex) paint, after the surface has been cleaned with a solution of sugar soap to remove any dirt or grease. If solvent-based (alkyd) paint has been used, this should be rubbed down with abrasive paper to provide a 'key' for the adhesive.

TILED WALLS A previously tiled surface is ideal to tile over, provided it is flat. Clean the surface and rub it down with silicon carbide abrasive paper to provide a 'key' for the adhesive.

Tiling over part-tiled walls will, of course, produce a pronounced ridge and it may be advisable to remove the old tiles first. If they are not that old, this should not be too difficult as you can simply lever them off with a bolster (wide) chisel and then remove the old adhesive with a scraper, chisel or disc sander. In older houses, however, tiles were often put on with cement mortar and getting them off can be a major exercise, requiring a hired percussion hammer and on breezeblock

walls you may well take part of the wall off with the mortar. Another way to avoid a noticeable ridge is to bring the untiled section of the wall up to the same level. This can be done by applying a sheet of plasterboard (dry wall or gypsum board) to it and then painting with emulsion (latex) paint before tiling the now flat entire wall.

PLASTER A bare plaster wall should be both smooth and flat and will provide an ideal surface for tiling. New plaster surfaces need to be left for at least a month before being tiled and you should make sure there are no splashes of plaster on the surface. Seal the wall with a stabilizing primer before applying adhesive. If an existing plaster surface is damaged, it will need to be repaired (see *Repairing Walls* opposite); if it is crumbling and falling away, it will need to be replastered, but check first that damp is not getting in from the outside of the wall (penetrating damp) or rising up from the ground as a result of a failed damp-proof course. Stop penetrating damp with a silicone water repellent applied on the outside of the wall and rising damp with a new chemical damp-proof course. Apply a damp sealer to the wall before tiling.

BRICK A bare brick or masonry wall will have to be plastered or covered with plasterboard before it is tiled. Alternatively, you could cover it with sheets of plywood, chipboard (particle board) or medium-density fibreboard (MDF), all of which will provide a suitable substrate for tiling.

Interesting effects can be achieved with wall tiles by using border tiles to 'frame' a mirror, by using shaped edge tiles and by laying tiles on the diagonal.

REPAIRING WALLS

It is essential that all wall surfaces be repared before tiling over them. Small cracks, holes and hollows can be made good with decorator's filler, applied with a filling knife and, if necessary, rubbed down with abrasive paper once it has set. If a hole is deep it may need more than one application of filler as trying to apply too much at once will result in the filler falling out.

Large areas of damage to a plaster wall can be repaired with plaster – either the traditional variety or a do-it-yourself plaster (which has the advantage of being able to fill deep holes in one go) – applied with a plasterer's float.

If the corner of a wall is damaged, secure a straight timber batten up against one side of the corner while you fill from the other side. Repeat on the other side of the corner when the first corner filled has dried.

FILLING HOLES

1 Use a flat-bladed filling knife to fill small holes with decorator's filler.

2 After the filler has dried, smooth the filled surface with abrasive paper.

REMOVING OLD TILES

1 To remove old wall tiles, use a bolster (wide) chisel inserted at the edge and tap gently with a mallet.

2 If the old adhesive is stuck firmly to the wall use an *old* wood chisel to scrape it off with the bevel of the chisel facing the wall (to stop it digging in).

3 Get the last bits off with a disc sander – wear protective gloves, goggles and a face mask when doing this.

FIXING CERAMIC WALL TILES

Whatever type of wall tile you are fixing, the basic procedure is the same and the first thing to decide is the width of the tiles at the edges.

If you are tiling from floor to ceiling, try to arrange it so that the edge tiles at the top and bottom are of equal size unless a whole tile can be used at the bottom and more than half a tile at the top. In a bathroom, it will look best if there is a row of whole tiles (or almost whole tiles) immediately over the bath, while in a kitchen it will look best if there is a similar row over the work surface.

The same goes for the side edge tiles too, and you will want to think about how tiles relate to other features – especially windows. The gauging stick will be invaluable here so that you can spend some time making sure that the tiles are 'centred' on the most prominent part of the wall and do not fall awkwardly at the edges and corners. Check in particular how ceramic tiles fall in relation to

cupboards and electric sockets in kitchens: cutting out the necessary L-shapes is not easy and you will want to keep this to a minimum.

Ceramic wall tiles need gaps between them which are filled with grout to give a neat appearance.

Some ceramic tiles have spacer lugs on them so that when they are put next to one another the correct gap is achieved; other ceramic tiles (known as 'universal' tiles) have angled edges so that when the backs of the tiles meet, there is a grouting gap left at the front edge. For square-edge ceramic tiles, you will have to create the grouting gaps.

The simplest method of achieving uniform grouting gaps is to insert matchsticks end on between the tiles. These can be removed once the adhesive has set. The alternative is to use a removable plastic spacer in the shape of a cross which fits into the junction between four tiles or a thin plastic cross-shaped spacer which fits in the same place, but is left in place (cut off the spacer arms where they protrude from edge tiles).

SETTING OUT

When you are happy with the proposed positions of the tiles, decide where you are going to start tiling (at the skirting board/ baseboard, say, or above the kitchen worktop) and secure a straight timber batten (furring strip) to the wall such that its top edge is at the position of the bottom edge of the *second* row of tiles. Secure the batten with screws or masonry nails and use a spirit level to ensure it is absolutely level, even if the skirting board or worktop is not. Make sure that the distance from the skirting board or worktop to the top of the batten is no more than one whole tile (allowing for the grouting gap).

Now nail a vertical batten to the wall so that its right-hand edge (if you are starting on the left) coincides with the position of the

This whole bathroom has been tiled with the same design of tile for a unified effect. Note the row of whole tiles immediately above the bath and the decorative border tiles which have been placed at 'picture rail' height.

first vertical row of tiles (or the second if the first row has to be cut or if tiling up to an end wall or cupboard edge). Secure this batten with screws or masonry nails, checking with a spirit level or plumb line that it is truly vertical even if the walls or cupboard are not. Again, make sure it is no more than a whole tile away from the end.

FIXING THE FIELD TILES

The main body of whole tiles – known as the 'field' – is fixed first and the adhesive is allowed to dry. Then the border or edge tiles are fitted.

Check with a try square that your two battens (furring strips) are at right angles (if not, adjust the one which is wrong) and start spreading tiling adhesive on the wall. If fixing ceramic tiles in an area which might get wet, always use a waterproof adhesive. Do not spread too much adhesive – around one square metre (10 square feet) is about right – and make sure that the adhesive is spread evenly over the surface.

Press the first tile into place in the corner between the two battens and then work outwards from this, one tile at a time. Push the tile firmly against the wall, so that adhesive is squeezed out at the edges until it is level. The adhesive allows you to 'slide' the tile on the wall to get it into the correct position.

For ceramic tiles which do not have spacer lugs or angled edges, use matchsticks or plastic spacers to provide the necessary gaps. As each tile is pressed into place, check with your gauging stick that it is in the correct place and by eye that it is straight. From time to time, hold a spirit level or straight-edge across the surface to ensure that the tiled surface is flat. Sometimes it may be necessary to remove a tile and to add adhesive to bring it up to the level of the other tiles or to remove adhesive to bring it back to the level.

Continue like this, spreading adhesive and fixing tiles, until all the whole field tiles are fixed. If you have to tile over a door or a bath (where you started at skirting board/baseboard level) or a skirting board (where you started at worktop level), fix another batten to support the bottom row of tiles to stop them slipping downwards under their own weight.

Make sure that all excess adhesive is wiped off the face of the tiles and not allowed to dry in place.

FIXING THE EDGE TILES

Leave the battens (furring strips) in place until the adhesive holding the field tiles has dried and then remove them carefully.

Now you can fit the edge tiles. With ceramic tiles, you need to check carefully which tiles to use. There are three different systems as follows.
- With angled-edge 'universal' tiles, each tile can be used either in the field or at an exposed edge.
- With square-edge tiles, you may find that all four edges have been glazed (also known as 'universal') in which case all tiles can be used everywhere, or that only some of the tiles in a box have one, two or four glazed edges for use on exposed edges and at exposed corners.
- Tiles with spacer lugs on each side are used as field tiles, while tiles with spacer lugs on three edges are rounded on the fourth side (RE tiles) for use at an exposed edge. Tiles with spacer lugs on two adjacent edges with two other adjacent edges rounded (REX tiles) are for use on exposed corners. You may need to buy these separately, so check carefully how many are needed.

An alternative way to finish off the edges of ceramic tiles is to use plastic edging strip,

Where there is a major feature in a room, such as a chimney breast, tiles should be centred on this. The effect has been enhanced here by the clever use of individual patterned tiles.

which fits under the last row of tiles. Versions are available which incorporate a sealing strip for use over baths.

Whole edge tiles are easy to fix – they simply fit up against the tiles you have already laid. But often you will have to cut edge tiles, remembering that with some ceramic tiles not to cut the rounded or glazed edge off.

To cut ceramic wall tiles, first measure the gap to be filled (allowing for the grouting gap). Then mark the tile, score across the face and finally 'snap' along the scored line – see *Cutting Ceramic Tiles* (page 80). Corner tiles will need to be cut twice – once for height and once for width. Always do the two operations separately.

To cut around obstacles such as electric sockets, windowsill ends or the corners of cupboards, mark the shape to be cut out either by measurement or by using a template or a profile gauge (see page 87) before making the cut.

TILING A WALL

1 To start tiling off, fix a vertical batten (furring strip) to mark the edge of the tiles (or one tile in, if against a wall).

2 Mark the position of the top of the lowest whole tile as a position guide for the horizontal batten.

3 Fix the horizontal batten in place and spread tiling adhesive over an area of about 1 square metre (10 square feet).

4 Start tiling in the corner between the two battens. Work outwards from the corner until all the field tiles have been fixed.

5 Fit the bottom row of tiles (cutting them if necessary) and apply grout to the gaps between the tiles with a squeegee.

6 Where the tiles in a bathroom meet the bath, use a silicone bath sealant to fill the gap between the tiles and the bath.

GROUTING

The gaps between ceramic tiles need to be filled with grout. If you have used a combined adhesive and grout to fix the tiles, this can be used for grouting as well.

Separate grouts usually need to be mixed up from powder and colour added if required. Plain and coloured ready-mixed grouts are also available.

To spread the grout, use a rubber squeegee, making sure it is pushed well into the gaps between the tiles. The squeegee can also be used to remove excess grout from the tile surface, but a damp sponge will also be needed for this. Remove excess grout regularly as it is difficult to get off once it has been allowed to harden.

When grout has been applied to all the gaps between tiles and has just started to harden, go along all the lines with a rounded wooden stick (or a special plastic grouting tool) to shape the grout in each gap to a concave rounded surface. Remove any excess grout as you go. Finally clean up the surface once more with a sponge and give it a polish with a dry cloth.

Where ceramic tiles are fitted above a kitchen worktop or a bath, do not grout the gap between the tiles and the worktop or bath. Instead, fill it with a silicone sealant which will provide more flexibility as the bath or worktop moves slightly.

USING EDGING STRIP

◁ **1** Edging strip is positioned under the last tile and is held in place when the tile is secured to the wall with adhesive.

▼ **2** To fit two pieces of edging strip at a corner, mitre the ends (cut at an angle of 45°) to make a neat join.

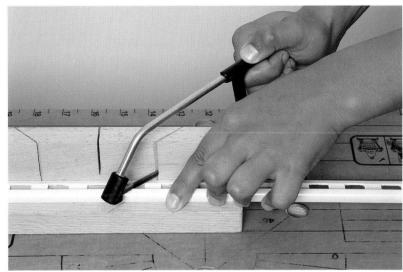

APPLYING GROUT

1 To start grouting, use a squeegee to force the grout into the gaps (here some narrow border tiles have been used as a decorative feature).

2 Use a rounded wooden stick or a special plastic grouting tool to produce neat concave joins between the tiles.

3 Finish off by removing all excess grout with a damp (but not wet) sponge and, finally, by polishing with a dry cloth.

CUTTING CERAMIC TILES

To score across the face of a ceramic tile, a special tool is required, either with a hardened sharp point or with a hardened wheel. You then 'snap' the tile either with a pair of tile snappers or by placing it over a pair of matchsticks lined up with the scored line and pressing down on either side of the tile. Alternatively, rest the tile on the edge of a square-topped work surface with the score lined up with the edge and 'snap' the tile by pressing down on the free side. At least one make of proprietary tile cutter has a special measuring device which is set to the whole gap to be filled and the tile is then scored in the correct place, allowing for the grouting gap. Most tile cutting machines have a 'breaker bar' built in to allow you to snap a tile after you have scored it.

Where only a small amount needs to be cut off a tile, score it as before, but use pliers or pincers to 'nibble' away the excess. When any tile has been cut, always use silicon carbide paper, a tile file, a carborundum block or an electric 'powerfile' fitted with a silicon carbide abrasive belt to smooth the edges.

To cut an L-shape out of a ceramic tile, use a tile saw to cut down one side of the L and then score and snap to remove the other side. To cut out shapes, such as the shape needed to fit around a windowsill end, first use a profile gauge or template to copy the shape (see page 87) and then a tile saw to cut out the shape. Smooth the cut edges as described above. Where only a small amount of tile needs to be removed, score a line on the surface (and more lines on the waste part of the tile) and then nibble the excess away with pincers or pliers.

1 To cut ceramic tiles in a straight line, first score the surface and then use a tile snapping tool.

2 Use a tile saw to cut out an awkward shape, such as to fit around a windowsill edge.

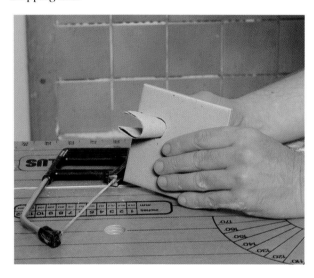

3 Smooth cut edges with silicon carbide abrasive paper.

4 Shapes can be removed from a ceramic tile by 'nibbling' with a pair of pincers or a pair of pliers.

OTHER TYPES OF WALL TILE

The step-by-step instructions given so far relate mainly to ceramic tiling. Other tiles are mostly fixed in the same way (though usually without the need to leave a grouting gap).

CORK TILES Cork tiles should always be fixed with equal borders on both sides, so fix the vertical batten (furring strip) in the centre and remove after one half of the wall has been fixed, using the edge tile of this half as a guide for the second half.

Special cork tile fixing adhesive needs to be used (unless they are self-adhesive) and the tiles are butt-jointed. Cut cork tiles with a trimming knife and use a wallpaper seam roller to press the edges in place.

MIRROR TILES These are fixed to the wall using self-adhesive pads. The surface must be absolutely flat so, if necessary, fit a sheet of plywood or MDF (medium-density fibreboard) over the area to be tiled on battens (furring strips) secured to the wall. To cut mirror tiles, use a glass cutter to score the line in one firm movement and snap the tile over a batten or a pair of matchsticks. Do not attempt curved cuts.

MOSAIC TILES These are fitted exactly like ceramic tiles, treating each block of mosaic as a single tile – check with the manufacturer's instructions to see whether a grouting gap needs to be left. To cut at the edges, you will have to cut each small tile individually and fit it in place. If there is a protective backing on the front of the tiles, leave it until the tiles have been fixed. Grout as for ceramic tiles.

FIXING MIRROR TILES

▲ **1** Mirror tiles are secured to the wall with self-adhesive pads.

▼ **2** Simply peel the backing paper off the pad and stick to the wall.

REPAIRING CERAMIC TILES

If a ceramic tile gets damaged, it is usually possible to remove just the damaged tile and to replace it. If the tile is on an exposed edge, it is relatively easy to remove, by sliding a bolster (wide) chisel under the edge and levering upwards. If, however, it is in the 'field', you will first have to drill holes in the tile and lever out some small pieces in order to get the blade of the bolster chisel in. It will help if you use a serrated grout remover on the grout lines around the tile first.

Once the tile has been removed, scrape out all the old adhesive, apply new adhesive to both the tile and the wall and push the new tile in place, making sure it is flush with its neighbours. Use spacers under the bottom edge to support the tile while the adhesive hardens. Finally, apply grouting all around the new tile as described on page 79.

REPLACING A BROKEN TILE

1 To remove a broken 'field' tile, first drill two lines of holes the length of the bolster (wide) chisel blade.

2 Use a strong putty knife (or an old wood chisel) to remove the pieces between the holes.

3 Insert the edge of the bolster chisel and gently ease away the tile.

4 Scrape away the old adhesive from behind the tile.

5 Apply new adhesive to both the wall and the tile and press the tile firmly in place ensuring it lies flat with its neighbours.

6 Use plastic spacers or matchsticks under the tile to support it while the adhesive dries. Grout the gap afterwards.

FITTING ACCESSORIES TO WALL TILES

You may want to fit things to ceramic wall tiles once the tiles are in place – knife sharpeners in a kitchen or a soap dish in the bathroom, for example.

No special equipment is needed here; the hole through the tile and into the wall can be drilled with a normal masonry drill and solid wallplugs or hollow wallplugs (depending on the type of wall) can be used to secure the fitting. But there are two points to watch.

The first is that a masonry drill will tend to skid about on the surface of the tile unless either you nick the tile at the position of the intended hole with a fine centre punch (this needs care to avoid cracking the tile) or use masking tape to cover the face of the tile (do this before marking the hole) and then drilling through this.

The second point is that a wallplug for solid walls should be pushed *right through* the tile, unless it is the type where the outer end of the plug does not expand. Otherwise, the screw expanding the wallplug will crack the tile. Hollow wallplugs (used on timber frame partition walls covered with plasterboard/dry wall or gypsum board) are not a problem as the wallplug (or toggle) expands *behind* the board.

FIXING A TOILET PAPER HOLDER TO THE WALL

1 To stop the drill skidding on the surface of the tile, apply masking tape before the position of the holes is marked.

2 On solid walls, make sure that wallplugs are pushed all the way through the tile into the solid masonry behind.

3 Fix the securing bracket to the wall using the screws supplied.

4 Secure the toilet paper holder by clipping it over the fixing brackets.

TILING FLOORS

One advantage of tiles rather than sheet materials for covering floors is that they are far more stable, neither expanding nor contracting in the same way as a sheet of the same material. This applies particularly to vinyl and lino flooring; tiles are also easier to put down than large unwieldy sheets.

Floor tiles offer more exciting and interesting design possibilities, too. These include mixing tiles with different patterns and colours (though not normally different materials) and adding border tiles of a contrasting pattern to the main body of tiles.

PREPARING FLOORS FOR TILING

Floor tiles need a dry flat surface and for most types of floor tile, solid concrete floors and suspended timber floors should be prepared and repaired as described in detail on pages 10–27. Use a floor primer to seal porous or dusty floors. 'Soft' floor tiles such as vinyl and cork need a smooth surface as any irregularities will show through the tiles and

bumps in the floor underneath will cause the covering to wear more quickly.

The exception is where you want to lay ceramic or quarry tiles on a suspended timber floor. To take the weight and to avoid flexing in use, the floor will need to be strengthened by fixing down sheets of 12 mm (½ in) exterior plywood sealed with two coats of wood primer. Do not use interior grade plywood as it could be affected by the moisture in the tiling adhesive. Fix the plywood down with screws at regular intervals, remembering to leave inspection hatches where necessary to gain access to pipes or electrical accessories, such as junction boxes, under the floorboards.

LAYING FLOOR TILES

All floor tiles are laid in roughly the same way, but there are differences, depending on whether the tiles are 'soft' (vinyl, cork, rubber, lino or carpet) or 'hard' (ceramic or quarry). The differences are in the type of adhesive used, the way in which the tiles are cut, and the way they are laid ('hard' tiles need a gap between them).

If you are laying tiles in a pattern, it is a good idea to draw a scale plan of the room (preferably on squared paper) and then to work out the pattern on that. This will avoid costly mistakes when actually putting down the tiles. A common tiling pattern is the 'chequerboard' design, where tiles of dark and light colour are set out alternately. But you could make up your own pattern and with removable carpet tiles even have a pattern which you could change (by replacing border tiles for example).

Whatever pattern or material you have chosen, the first thing to do will be to find the centre of the room, which is where floor tiling always starts.

A traditional look has been achieved here by using hand-painted insets with heraldic designs and richly coloured terracotta floor tiles.

A patterned border can give a much more decorative finish to vinyl or lino tiles.

SETTING OUT

To find the centre of the room, first find the centre points of the two longest walls, fix a chalk line between these at floor level and 'snap' it down on the floor. Now measure the centre point of this line and fix a chalk line between the two shorter walls passing through this point, but exactly at right angles to the first line – check with a tile or a builder's square. When you have adjusted this line so that it is at right angles to the first *and* passes through the centre point, 'snap' it down. You now have your starting point.

If the room has a distinctive feature – such as a fireplace, a bay window or a bathroom vanity unit – you will want to centre the tiles on this rather than on the room dimensions. To do this, snap a third chalk line from the centre of the feature, parallel with the line you have already made, to get your new starting point.

There are four possible positions to lay the first tile: the one you use will be determined by the width left at the edges where you will have to cut tiles to fit. Ideally, the two edge tiles should be the same size and not less than half a tile.

Check your starting position by making a 'dry' run in both directions, using your actual tiles (or a gauging stick with ceramic or quarry tiles) and adjust the position of the central tiles until you have got the edges equal – avoid having thin pieces of tile at the edges as they will be difficult to stick down.

Tiles can also be laid diagonally rather than parallel with the room walls. To set this out, mark the centre point as before and place a tile so that each of its corners is over the two chalk lines. Draw around this tile and then continue the lines out across the room. Now draw a line parallel with each pair of lines, through the centre point.

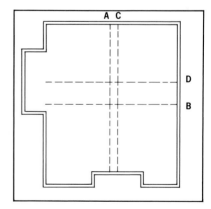

SETTING OUT

If the room has prominent features, adjust the centre lines (A and B) to line up on a chimney breast (C) or a bay window (D).

LAYING 'SOFT' FLOOR TILES

Vinyl, lino, cork, rubber and carpet tiles are all laid in the same way, the only difference being in the adhesive used – note that many tiles these days are self-adhesive and require only the removal of the backing paper to stick them down.

FITTING THE FIELD TILES

First of all the centre point must be established as described on page 85 and the position of the first tile (the 'key' tile) determined. Place this down dry (or with the backing paper still attached) in the chosen position, checking that this is exactly in line with your chalk lines and that it looks right in the room. Now draw carefully around this and extend the lines beyond the edge of the tile (otherwise you will not be able to see the lines when you come to lay the tile).

Spread adhesive on the floor using the plastic spreader supplied with the tile adhesive (or remove the backing for a self-adhesive tile) and put one side of the tile down on the marked line, 'rolling' the rest of the tile down flat. If you get it wrong, pull it up again immediately and start again – unlike ceramic tile adhesive, there is no adjustment possible. Note that with rubber tiles the recommended adhesive is applied to both the tile and to the floor.

Now work outwards from this tile, laying one tile at a time. When spreading adhesive on the floor do not cover more than about a square metre (10 square feet) at a time. Make sure that each tile is put down in line and that it is butt-jointed closely to the next tile. If any adhesive squeezes up between the joints, remove it at once with a damp cloth or a cloth dampened with white (mineral) spirit (check the adhesive manufacturer's instructions). Where the tiles have decorative markings, it is usual to lay them 'cross-grained' – that is, with the markings on adjacent tiles at right angles to each other.

Continue laying whole floor tiles until you get to the edges of the room, where the tiles need to be cut.

FITTING THE EDGE TILES

Around the edges of the room, you will have to cut each individual tile to the correct size.

The way to cut an edge tile accurately is to lay a whole tile exactly on top of the last whole tile to have been laid in a row and then place a third whole tile on top of it, so that it is lined up with the middle tile, but meets the wall along its edge. Now draw a pencil line along the opposite edge of the top tile. This is your cutting line.

Next take the middle tile and cut or break it along the line. The part of the middle tile furthest from the wall is the edge tile and it will fit the space exactly.

You can adapt the same procedure to use up a part tile (one that has already been cut). To do this, line up the uncut edge of the tile with the *back* edge of the bottom tile (that is, with the cut edge facing the wall) to mark the second cutting line.

At corners, you will have to repeat the procedure twice. So you do not get confused, write A on the floor against one wall and B against the other and then write A and B on the bottom side of the tile to show which way round it goes.

For tiles which have been laid *diagonally*, you must modify the procedure by making a rectangular hardboard template, the length of which is equal to the diagonal dimension of the tile (for a square tile, 1.414 times its length). This template is then placed against the wall with a whole tile placed on top of **the next to last tile in each row.**

To lay the edge tile, spread more adhesive (or remove the backing paper) and simply stick the tile down. It is probably easiest to do this one tile at a time as you go, since the tiles will usually vary slightly in size and you do not want to get them mixed up.

This bold design features plain lino tiles surrounded by border strips in contrasting colours.

FITTING AROUND OBSTACLES

The four main 'obstacles' you are going to meet with floor tiles are square cupboards (or vanity units in bathrooms), curved pedestal basins and WC pans in bathrooms, doorways and pipes passing up through the floor.

A square cupboard is the easiest to negotiate and here you use the same technique as described opposite for cutting edge and corner tiles.

Curved obstacles are more difficult and the best method is to cut a paper template to the correct shape. Make the template slightly larger than a tile so you can mark on it where the two edges of the tile will come and fold the template back along these two edges. Fold or cut the template around the curved object (make inward cuts to help you do this) until you have reproduced the shape exactly (be prepared to have more than one go at this). Then place the template over the tile, lining it up with the edges, and draw your cutting line, which can then be cut with a trimming knife or scissors.

At doorways, hold the tile against the doorway from both sides and mark on the edges where the main lines of the door frame and architrave moulding will come on the tile. Then use a profile gauge to reproduce the exact shape of the moulding and transfer this to the tile. It is a good idea to try this out on a tile-sized piece of card first, so you can check the measurements are correct before cutting the tile. When you have got it right on the card, use the card as a template for marking and cutting the tile.

To fit 'soft' tiles around pipes coming up through the floor, cut the tile to the correct size (if it is an edge tile) and then hold it against the pipe on two sides, first parallel with the last whole tile and second against the wall, so that you can mark on the tile where the two edges of the pipe fall. Then using a try square, continue these lines across the tile until they meet and the square in the centre is exactly where the pipe will pass through. Mark the centre of this square and drill or cut out a circle slightly larger than the pipe. Make a single cut from the hole to the edge of the tile which will be against the wall and the tile can now be manoeuvred into place, passing the pipe through this cut and into its hole.

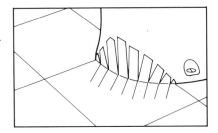

DEALING WITH CURVED OBSTACLES

A paper template can be used to reproduce the shape of curved objects.

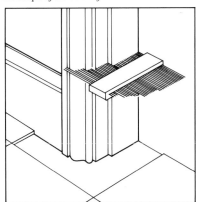

DOORWAYS

Transfer the shape of a doorway moulding on to a tile using a profile gauge.

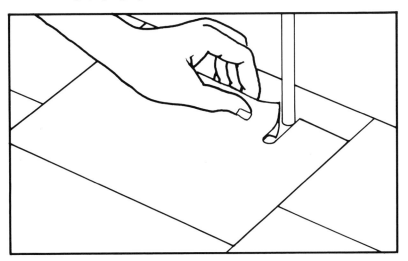

PIPES

Cut a round hole for the pipe and slit it to the edge of the tile.

FINISHING OFF

Soft floor tiles should be rolled with a 68 kg (150 lb) floor roller (which you can hire) to make sure that they are absolutely flat. If the tile comes with a protective covering, wait until all the tiles have been laid before peeling this off.

Most 'soft' floor tiles need no further treatment once laid, but unsealed cork tiles should be given two coats of polyurethane floor varnish a day or so after they have been laid (use a single sealing coat on sealed cork tiles).

LAYING CORK TILES

1 Before laying 'soft' floor tiles, such as cork, prepare the floor surface and where necessary cover it with sheets of hardboard cut to size.

2 Nail the hardboard down with hardboard nails or with 'ring shank' nails.

3 Find the centre of the room and start tiling here so that edge tiles are equal width and not less than half a tile. Work outwards, spreading adhesive as you go (unless the tiles are self-adhesive).

4 Lay all the whole tiles up to both edges.

5 Cut the edge tiles by laying a whole tile on top of the last whole tile and a third whole tile against the wall to give the cutting line.

6 Spread more adhesive and fit the edge tiles one at a time as you go. Corner tiles will need cutting twice.

7 Any adhesive seeping through to the surface of the tile must be removed immediately with a cloth dampened with water or white (mineral) spirit.

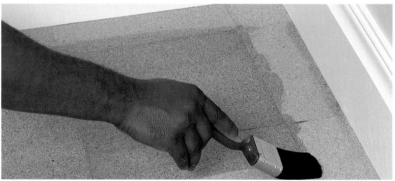

8 For unsealed cork floor tiles, apply two coats of floor varnish once the tiles have all been laid and the adhesive has dried.

LAYING BORDER TILES

You can create a very interesting effect by laying some narrow patterned border tiles (vinyl or lino) with your main flooring tiles. They have the effect of 'framing' the main floor and can either be laid at the extreme edge or just inside the edge so that there are plain tiles both inside and outside the border and the corners of the border join up.

The diamond lino border tiles come in lengths which have been cut around one diamond so that they fit together. The two outer strips have been extended (to protect the points of the diamond), so need to be cut off before two strips can be laid together.

If the border tiles are to be laid at the edges, you lay these first followed by the main flooring; if they are to be laid away from the wall, you lay the main body of tiles first, then the border and finally the tiles between the border and the wall. You will need to position the border 'dry' exactly where you want it and then mark the inside edge with pencil (or strike a chalk line) to act as a guideline to which the main floor covering will be laid.

The border tiles themselves are laid in exactly the same way as normal floor tiles, the only exception being how they are joined at the corners. Here, you will need to remove a small amount of the covering strip and cut carefully around the pattern to give a neat join. Do this 'dry' and then spread adhesive and lay the border tiles. Choose the most prominent corner to make the neatest join. Finish by peeling off the covering strip and rolling the whole floor (especially the border) with a 68 kg (150 lb) floor roller.

LAYING LINO BORDER TILES

1 Lay the border tiles 'dry' in the final position and draw a mark along their inside edges.

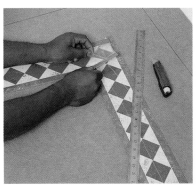

2 In order to cut the corners, first peel off a small amount of the protective covering.

3 Cut carefully around the pattern so that the two corner pieces meet at right angles.

4 Lay the border strip in adhesive along the marked line, pressing it firmly down into place.

5 Fit the main body of tiles and finally peel off the protective covering and roll the whole floor.

LAYING 'HARD' FLOOR TILES

The way in which you lay 'hard' floor tiles (mainly ceramic, quarry and terracotta tiles) is slightly different from the method used in laying 'soft' floor tiles; you need to leave a gap between the tiles and a different adhesive is used. Cutting the tiles will also be much more difficult. Terracotta tiles are laid in the same way as quarry tiles.

The floor itself will need to be reasonably level if it is solid. Floor levelling compound can be used with ceramic tiles, but need not be used for quarry tiles – the thick cement-based adhesive will allow for some discrepancy. Suspended timber floors will need to be strengthened with 12 mm (½ in) exterior-grade plywood or the floorboards can be removed and replaced with chipboard (particle board) sheet (see pages 20–21). In either case, remember to leave inspection hatches if required.

FITTING THE TILES

The tiles should be set out in the way described on page 85 – that is, first find the centre of the room and then work out how wide the edge tiles will be, adjusting the position of the centre tile so that you get equal edges. The edge tiles should be at least half a tile's width.

Ceramic tiles and machine-made quarry tiles can be laid on a bed of adhesive as recommended by the manufacturers (a cement-based adhesive for quarry tiles). If the ceramic tiles do not have spacer lugs, you can buy special plastic spacers – or, if you want to make a feature of the grouting lines, improvise some wider spacers from, say, short lengths of 6 mm (¼ in) dowelling rod. For quarry tiles, use short lengths of 6 mm (¼ in) timber to produce the grouting gaps.

When you have worked out the spacing of the tiles, secure a timber batten (furring strip) across the centre of the room and use this as a guide for laying the tiles. Lay around one square metre (10 square feet) of adhesive at a time and press the tiles into place, with the correct gaps between them. Check that the lines of tiles are straight and that the gaps between them are continuous. Lay all the whole tiles like this on half the floor, remove the batten and then tile the other half of the floor. Allow 24 hours for the adhesive to set before cutting and fitting the edge tiles – note

that you should not walk on the tiles during this time, so if the room is one in constant use (such as a kitchen or bathroom) tile one half of the room one day, and the other half the next day. Finish off by using the recommended grout.

Hand-made quarry tiles vary in thickness and normally need to be laid on a 'slurry' of neat cement and water on top of a level sand and cement screed. Press the tiles down into the slurry using spacer strips 6 mm (¼ in) wide, checking regularly with a straight-edge that the tiles are all flat. If any tiles are above the level, tamp them down with a block of wood; if any are below the level, lever them out and add more cement slurry.

Continue like this until all the whole tiles are laid and then leave for at least 12 hours for the mortar to set. Then cut and fit the edge tiles.

CUTTING 'HARD' TILES

To measure up for 'hard' edge tiles, simply use a steel tape measure to find the distance between the last whole tile and the wall (measure both sides as the gap may taper) and transfer the measurements to the tile, allowing for the grouting gap.

Ceramic floor tiles and quarry tiles are thicker than ceramic wall tiles and so are more difficult to cut. You will certainly need a tile cutting machine to do the job (this can be hired); for cutting curves (to fit round a wash stand, say), a good tool to use is an angle grinder (which can also be hired) fitted with a masonry cutting disc.

To fit hard tiles around a pipe passing up through the floor, mark the position and size of the pipe on the tile as described on page 47, drill a hole slightly larger in the tile and then cut the tile in two, fitting one half either side of the pipe (see diagram below).

FILLING THE GAPS

The gaps between ceramic floor tiles are filled with grout in the same way as ceramic wall tiles (see page 79).

For quarry tiles, use the recommended grout or a dry mix of one part cement to one part sand to pack the bottom of the joint and then use a grouting mix of cement and water to finish off. Use a heavy-duty squeegee to push the base mix and the grouting mix into the joints. As this is drying, fashion it into a gentle concave shape with a short length of flexible rubber hosing. Finish off by polishing the joints with a damp sponge.

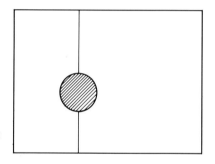

PIPES

To fit a 'hard' tile around a pipe, cut through the tile after making a hole for the pipe.

LAYING TERRACOTTA TILES

1 To lay terracotta tiles, use a cement-based adhesive spread to a thickness of 6 mm (¼ in).

2 Smooth out the adhesive with a notched trowel to form ridges.

3 Press the tiles down into place, leaving grouting gaps between them.

4 Check the size of the gaps with spacer bars and, if necessary, slide the tiles up to keep the gaps even.

5 To cut curved shapes in terracotta tiles, use an angle grinder fitted with a masonry cutting disc.

6 Cover terracotta tiles with a solution of boiled linseed oil, applied with a long-pile roller.

FINISHING OFF

Ceramic tiles need no further finishing apart from wiping off the grouting (*before* it sets hard) with a damp sponge and polishing with a dry cloth. For quarry tiles, the traditional finish is wax polish, but these days an alternative is to rub or roll the surface with a solution of boiled linseed oil.

Opposite: *Large-sized patterned ceramic floor tiles are here used to great effect with complementary borders surrounded by plain tiles to produce a panelled design.*

7 Force a cement and water mix down into the gaps between the tiles with a heavy-duty squeegee.

8 Finish off the gaps with a length of flexible rubber hosing to give a gentle concave shape.

STOCKISTS AND SUPPLIERS

BASIC TOOLS AND EQUIPMENT

Black & Decker Ltd
Westpoint
The Grove
Slough
Berkshire SL1 1QQ
0753 511234

Hobbs & Co Ltd
88 Blackfriars Road
London SE1 8HA
071-928 1891

H S S Hire Group Ltd
25 Willow Lane
Mitcham
Surrey CR4 9AR
081-685 9900

Mosley-Stone
3 Morgan Way
Bowthorpe Industrial Estate
Bowthorpe
Norwich
Norfolk
NR5 9JJ
0603 743665

W C Youngman
Stane Street
Slinford
Horsham
West Sussex RH13 7RD
0403 790456

CARPET ACCESSORIES

Gripperrods plc
Wyrley Brook Park
Walkmill Lane
Bridgtown
Cannock
Staffordshire WS11 3XA
0922 417777

CARPETS, MATTINGS AND RUGS

The Carpet Bureau
911 Fulham Road
London SW6 5HU
071-371 9600

Crucial Trading
The Market Hall
Craven Arms
Shropshire SY7 8ZZ
0588 673666

Huega UK Ltd
The Gate House
Gate House Way
Aylesbury
Buckinghamshire HP19 3DL
0296 393244

Kosset Carpets Ltd
Toftshaw Lane
Bradford
West Yorkshire BD4 6QW
0274 681881

Nice Irma's Ltd
Spring House
Spring Place
London NW5 3BH
071-284 0544

Tomkinsons Carpets Ltd
PO Box 11
Duke Place
Kidderminster
Worcestershire DY10 2JR
0562 820006

Woodward Grosvenor & Co Ltd
Stourvale Mills
Green Street
Kidderminster
Worcestershire DY10 1AT
0562 820020

CORK

Siesta Cork Tile Co
Unit 21
Tait Road
Gloucester Road
Croydon
Surrey CR0 2DP
081-683 4055

Westco Floormaker Ltd
Penarth Road
Cardiff
South Glamorgan CF1 7YN
0222 233926

Wicanders (GB) Ltd
Stoner House
Kilnmead
Crawley
West Sussex RH10 2BG
0293 527700

LINO

Forbo Nairn Ltd
Woodside Road
Glenrothes
Fife KY7 4AF
0592 759666

TILES

Castelnau Tiles
175 Church Road
Barnes
London SW13 9HR
081-741 2452

Corres Mexican Tiles
219–221 Chiswick High Road
London W4
081-994 0215

Fired Earth Tiles plc
Twyford Mill
Oxford Road
Adderbury
Banbury
Oxfordshire OX17 3HP
0295 812088

H & R Johnson Tiles Ltd
Highgate Tile Works
Tunstall
Stoke-on-Trent
Staffordshire ST6 4JX
0782 575575

The Merchant Tiler
Twyford Mill
Oxford Road
Adderbury
Banbury
Oxfordshire OX17 3HP
0295 812179

Pilkingtons Tiles Ltd
PO Box 4
Clifton Junction
Manchester
Lancashire M27 2LP
061-794 2024

Dennis Ruabon Ltd
Hafod Tileries
Ruabon
Wrexham
Clwyd LL14 6ET
0978 843484

TILING ACCESSORIES AND ADHESIVES

Building Adhesives Ltd
Longton Road
Trentham
Stoke-on-Trent
Staffordshire
ST4 8JB
0782 659921

Cintride Ltd
Ashford Road Works
Bakewell
Derbyshire DE4 1GL
0629 812513

Evode Ltd
Common Road
Stafford
Staffordshire
ST16 3EH
0785 57755

Homelux Products Ltd
Block 4
Blackbrook Business Park
Dudley
West Midlands DY2 0XQ
0384 455600

Douglas Kane
Carlyon Road
Atherstone
Warwickshire CV9 1LQ
0827 714511

Martek Ltd
PO Box 20
Redruth
Cornwall TR15 2UF
0209 219911

Onduline Building Products Ltd
Eardley House
182–184 Campden Hill Road
London W8 7AS
071-727 0533

Plasplugs Ltd
Wetmore Road
Burton-on-Trent
Staffordshire DE14 1SD
0283 30303

Vitrex Ltd
Kilnhouse Lane
Lytham St Annes
Lancashire FY8 3DU
0253 721291

VINYL

The Amtico Company Ltd
17 St George Street
London W1R 9DE
071-629 6258

**Armstrong World
Industries Ltd**
Armstrong House
38 Market Square
Uxbridge
Middlesex UB8 1NG
0895 251122

Forbo Nairn Ltd
Woodside Road
Glenrothes
Fife KY7 4AF
0592 759666

Gerland Ltd
90 Crawford Street
London
W1H 2AP
071-723 6601

James Halstead Ltd
Retail Division
PO Box 3
Radcliffe New Road
Whitefield
Manchester
Lancashire M25 7NR
061-766 3781

Marley Floors Ltd
Dickley Lane
Lenham
Maidstone
Kent ME17 2DE
0622 858877

Tarkett Ltd
Poyle House
PO Box 173
Blackthorne Road
Colnbrook
Slough
Berkshire SL3 0AZ
0753 684533

WOOD

**Campbell Marson and
Company Ltd**
Unit 34
Wimbledon Business Centre
Riverside Road
London SW17 0BA
081-879 1909

Junckers Ltd
Wheaton Court
Commercial Centre
Wheaton Road
Witham
Essex CM8 3UJ
0376 517512

Kährs (UK) Ltd
Unit 1
Timberlaine Estate
Quarry Lane
Chichester
West Sussex PO19 2FJ
0243 784417

Tarkett Ltd
Poyle House
PO Box 173
Blackthorne Road
Colnbrook
Slough
Berkshire SL3 0AZ
0753 684533

Vigers Floor Ltd
Vigers House
North Weald Airfield
North Weald
Epping
Essex CM16 6AA
0992 523035

Westco Floormaker Ltd
Penarth Road
Cardiff
South Glamorgan
CF1 7YN
0222 233926

Wicanders (GB) Ltd
Stoner House
Kilnmead
Crawley
West Sussex RH10 2BG
0293 527700

NORTH AMERICA

BASIC TOOLS AND EQUIPMENT

Black & Decker
Communications Department
702 East Joppa Road
Towson
Maryland 21286

**Robert Bosch Power Tool
Corporation**
100 Bosch Blvd
New Bern
North Carolina 28562

Home Depot
2727 Paces Ferry Road
Atlanta
Georgia 30339
(404) 433–8211

J C Penney
1301 Avenue of the Americas
New York
New York 10019
(800) 222–6161

Porter Cable Corporation
4825 Highway 45 North
Jackson
Tennessee 38302

Sears Roebuck
Sears Tower
Chicago
Illinois 60684
(800) 366–3000

Skil Corporation
4300 West Peterson Avenue
Chicago
Illinois 60646

True Value Hardware
(800) 621–6025

FLOORING PRODUCTS AND TILES

**American Olean Tile
Company**
1000 Cannon Avenue
Lansdale
Pennsylvania 19446–0271
(215) 855–1111

Armstrong World Industries
PO Box 3001
Lancaster
Pennsylvania 17603
(800) 233–3823

Crossville Ceramics
Box 1168
Crossville
Tennessee 38557
(615) 484–2110

Home Depot
2727 Paces Ferry Road
Atlanta
Georgia 30339
(404) 433–8211

Kentile Floors, Inc
58 Second Avenue
Brooklyn
New York 11215

Latco (tiles)
2948 Gleneden Street
Los Angeles
California 90039
(213) 664–1171

J C Penney
1301 Avenue of the Americas
New York
New York 10019
(800) 222–6161

Rickel Home Centers
200 Milik Street
Caateret
New Jersey 07008
(201) 499–3000

Sears Roebuck
Sears Tower
Chicago
Illinois 60684
(800) 366–3000

Stark Carpet Corporation
977 Third Avenue
New York
New York 10022

Summitville Tiles, Inc
Box 73
Summitville
Ohio 43962
(216) 223–1511

True Value Hardware
(800) 621–6025

GLOSSARY

Baluster The vertical spindles of a staircase. Together with handrail (banister rail) makes up the *banisters*.

Baseboard *see* Skirting board

Batten (furring strip) A generic name for a strip of timber, often used for support.

Batts Small semi-rigid pieces of insulation material used to insulate cavity walls or floors.

Block flooring Timber flooring consisting of individual wooden blocks, usually laid in a herringbone pattern. Also known as *parquet*.

Bonded carpet Carpet with the fibres secured in an adhesive backing.

Bullnose stair The bottom stair of a staircase which is wider than the remainder and curves around the main *newel post* supporting the banisters.

Chipboard (particle board) Man-made board consisting of wood chips in glue. Used as sheet flooring.

Damp-proof membrane An impervious layer installed in solid floors to prevent damp rising.

Dry wall *see* Plasterboard

Expansion gap A small space left at the edges of a timber floor to allow for expansion of the wood. Usually covered by skirting board (baseboard) or moulding.

Expansion strip A cork strip used to put in an exposed expansion gap.

Fibreboard A man-made board consisting of wood fibres bonded together. Medium-density fibreboard (MDF) is generally stronger and smoother than chipboard (particle board).

Furring strip *see* Batten

Gripper strip Wooden strip with angled metal spikes fixed around the edges of a room to secure carpet.

Gypsum board *see* Plasterboard

Hardboard A light-duty *fibreboard*, used underneath floor coverings on uneven floors.

Latex adhesive Used for repairing carpets.

Lino (linoleum) A flooring material made from natural ingredients (linseed oil, cork and wood).

Mosaic flooring Generally timber flooring consisting of thin 'fingers' of timber arranged in a basketweave pattern and mounted on a backing or

wired and glued together.

Mosaic tiles Small ceramic tiles arranged on a backing material.

Mortar A mixture of cement, sand and water used for screeding floors and for filling the joints between quarry tiles (when laid on a screed).

Newel The post at the bottom (and top) of stairs used to support the *banisters*.

Nosing The curved edge at the front of a stair tread.

Oleo-resin A pine gum obtained by distilling dead wood or by bleeding the living tree. Used for sealing wood floors.

Parquet *see* Block flooring

Particle board *see* Chipboard

Paving bricks Special bricks, suitable for use on floors (also known as brick pavers).

Plasterboard (dry wall or gypsum board) Solid gypsum plaster sandwiched between paper. Nailed to joists for ceilings and to upright timbers (studs) for internal walls.

Plywood Real-wood board consisting of three or more thin sheets (plys) glued together with the grain of adjacent sheets running at right angles to one another for strength.

Polypropylene Inexpensive man-made fibre used in carpets.

Profile gauge Thin strips of plastic mounted next to one another in a holder. When pushed against a moulding, the plastic strips move to take up the moulding shape which can then be transferred to a flooring material.

Quadrant (quarter round) moulding Hardwood moulding with a cross-section the shape of one quarter of a circle. Used for covering expansion gaps in wooden flooring. Small sizes sometimes known as 'quadrant beading'.

Riser The vertical parts of a staircase fitted at the back of each *tread*.

Rising damp The natural tendency of moisture to rise in floors and walls. Combated by a damp-proof membrane in floors and a damp-proof course in walls.

Scotia moulding A timber moulding with a concave curved front and a square back, used for covering

expansion gaps in timber flooring.

Screed A thin level concrete layer on top of a concrete slab in timber floors.

Secret nailing A method of securing tongued-and-grooved flooring such that the nail put through the tongue of one piece is covered by the groove of the next piece.

Shellac A natural resin formed by the lac insect. Used with wax for sealing timber floors.

Skirting board (baseboard) A length of timber secured to a wall at the bottom for decoration and to conceal the gap between the wall and the floor.

Slurry A fluid cement-water mix used for securing man-made quarry tiles.

Spacer lug A protrusion on the sides of ceramic tiles to achieve the correct grouting gap.

Square-edge boards Timber floorboards with square edges (ie not *tongued-and-grooved*) which are simply pushed up against one another, but can sometimes leave a gap.

Strip flooring Thin or thick timber flooring available in tongued-and-grooved strips which give the impression of floorboards.

Suspended floor A floor consisting of timber floorboards or chipboard (particle board) sheet flooring mounted on floor joists.

Threshold strip A metal bar used to finish the edge of carpet or sheet flooring at a doorway.

Tongued-and-grooved A way of finishing the edges of floorboards (or other timber flooring) such that the tongue on one piece fits into the groove in the adjacent piece with no gap.

Treads The horizontal parts of a staircase, fitting in front of the *risers*.

Universal tiles Either ceramic wall tiles which are glazed on all four edges (so can be used anywhere) or ceramic wall tiles which are angled from front to back so that when pushed together a grouting gap is left on the front face.

Vinyl An abbreviation for polyvinyl chloride. Used as a flooring material.

Wallplates The horizontal pieces of timber on sleeper walls on which floor joists rest.

Woodblock flooring *see* Block flooring

Woodstrip flooring *see* Strip flooring

INDEX

PICTURE CREDITS

The authors and publishers would like to thank the following
companies and their PR agencies for the loan of photographs used
in this book.

The Amtico Company Ltd: Pages 6/7, 33 tr.
Campbell Marson and Company Ltd: page 32 b.
Corres Mexican Tiles: pages 33 b, 77.
Crucial Trading: pages 31 t, 33 tl.
Dulux: pages 32 t, 34, 35 b, 38, 39.
Fired Earth Tiles plc: pages 2, 28, 29, 37 t, 74.
Forbo-Nairn Ltd: front cover, pages 65, 86.
Heuga UK Ltd: pages 30 t, 50.
H & R Johnson Tiles Ltd/Cristal: back cover, pages 37 hr, 68, 76, 90.
Junckers Ltd: pages 10, 44, 47 bl, 48.
Kosset Carpets Ltd: page 56/57.
The Merchant Tiler: pages 37 bl, 73, 84.
Nice Irma's Ltd: page 31 b.
Tomkinsons Carpets Ltd: pages 36, 55, 62.
Wicanders (GB) Ltd: page 30 b.
Woodward Grosvenor: pages 35 t, 58.

Key: t = top; b = bottom; l = left; r = right; c = centre.

ACKNOWLEDGEMENTS

The authors and publishers would like to thank the following
companies and their PR agencies for their advice and the loan
and/or provision of materials and equipment used in this book. See
Stockists and Suppliers for addresses and telephone numbers.

Black & Decker Ltd
The Carpet Bureau
Crucial Trading
Fired Earth Tiles plc
H S S Hire Group Ltd
H & R Johnson Tiles Ltd/Cristal
Junckers Ltd
The Merchant Tiler
Mosley-Stone
Plasplugs Ltd
W C Youngman

Anness Publishing would also like to thank Roger and Samuel and
the other private individuals who helped in the realisation of this
book.